To the women who came before me,
Lisa Ann Liimatta
Alyce Julianna Riutta
Hilda Henriette Anderson
Ida Josefina Kuru
Ella Kristina Nilomaa
Margareta Laurinytar Vittikko
Ella Johansdotter, born 1769

LIVE YOUR

YES

LIFE

Get What You Want Without Being Stopped by Money, Time, or Approval

Written by Kaela Gedda
with Lisa Liimatta

HU
HOUSE
PUBLISHING

HEARTS UNLEASHED HOUSE PUBLISHING

For information about special discounts for bulk purchases contact:
hearts@heartsunleashed.com

Manufactured in the United States of America
Library of Congress Cataloging-in-Publication Data Gedda, Kaela.

Summary:

Live Your YES Life is a must-read manual for the person who's been dreaming of a new possibility for themselves, and isn't entirely sure on how or even if that dream could become a reality.

Kaela becomes your personal Life Coach throughout the book, taking you through a process of uncovering what it is that you want most, and then opening new paths of how you can choose that for yourself without being stopped by money, time, or approval.

Rather than putting your dreams on the back burner, or letting circumstances take the lead, you'll be supported to say YES to you, now.

Throughout the book you'll participate in exercises to:
- Gain clarity on your purpose
- Identify the desires and dreams calling to you now
- Believe in yourself
- Uncover roadblocks and solutions
- Connect with your worth
- Process your emotions
- Discover your unique Wealth Code
- Empower your relationship with money and time
- Create your Joy Wheel
- Trust yourself

Live Your YES Life gives you the tools to put YOU in the driver's seat and get what you want while being connected to your worth, possibilities, and a new depth of self-trust.

ISBN: 979-8-9882783-8-2

[1. Personal & Professional Development. 2. Self-Help. 3. Success. 4. Business. 5. Visualization. 6. Motivation. 7. Inspiration.]

ACKNOWLEDGMENTS

First, thank you GOD for writing this book through me. Thank you for choosing me to be the channel this message flowed through. I know that when we started this Divine Assignment I had some resistance, and I am grateful that you made it clear that I was to answer this call. Writing this book has been an incredible experience of trust and being obedient to your plan. I find that you call me so much greater than I call myself.

Thank you to my parents, Lisa Liimatta and Brian Gedda. Mom, we've been partners for 34 years and counting, which makes our business partnership all the more sacred. Thank you for your contributions to my life, to our work, and to this book. Dad, I am largely the woman that I am because of you. This book was swiftly written as a summary of the experiences that I've had over the years, all of which you have contributed to by believing in me.

Thank you to my husband, Tom. You are the gold star of partners. Thank you for the way that you support me and our family so that I have the space to create. Thank you for trusting me completely since the start of our relationship. Murray, Millie, and Melvin—you are the best dogs and brought me joy, laughter, and much needed breaks during this process. I love you, babies!

Thank you to each and every one of my clients. Getting to be your Life Coach is an honor. I am so grateful for the way that you show up in your power, vulnerable and full of dedication to living *your* YES life. I wrote this book because of you, for you, and in celebration of you. You are my muses.

Thank you to Abigail and her outstanding team at Hearts Unleashed House Publishing. It was so fun to call you one day and say, "I wrote a book! Can we publish it in two months?!" and it was even more fun to hear you say, "YES! We've been waiting for this day." I am so grateful for your guidance, wisdom, and heart.

Thank you to all of my pre readers who answered my call and supported me with an incredibly fast turnaround: Kate, Erin, Molly, and Claudia-Sam. Your feedback, support, and edits made this book so much better, and now it is the work of us all. I love you, friends!

TABLE OF CONTENTS

Chapter 1

Agreements

I did not want to write this book. If I am going to be honest with you for this entire book, and I am, it means I need to start with sentence one. I do not necessarily like business or personal development books. I read them, I take on the practices offered with spirit, I allow my life to be changed by them, I refer them to others, but they are not my preferred genre.

I would just rather sink my teeth into a great fiction. Give me a woman time traveling back to the 1800s or some good vampire drama any day.

I have two Bachelor of Arts degrees. One in English and the other in Communications. I am a writer. I love writing. I always knew that someday I would write a book. But I never wanted to put pressure on myself about what or when. When asked, "Why don't you write a book?" I always replied, "I'm going to let the book write itself. I'll answer the door when it knocks."

This book knocked. I peeked out the window and said, "No thanks, I really don't want to write a business or self-development book." It kept knocking.

I want you to know this for a few reasons. One, my intention for writing this book isn't to become a best-selling author or win an award. Now, I am totally open to that possibility and welcome abundance in all of its forms, but it's not my intention.

My intention is to say some bold things to you, things other people might not have the courage to say, things that you may not have known to consider for yourself.

My intention is to arm you with perspectives, resources, and a look inside of yourself so that you can transform your life if you so choose.

My intention is to partner with you so that you can have what you want, without getting stopped by time, money, or approval.

The second reason I am telling you this is because while I absolutely embrace my identity as a writer, I'm really sharing these words in my role as a life coach. This is my profession, it is my gift. Over the past eight years I have coached hundreds of clients, completed numerous advanced training certifications, and fallen more and more in love with the transformative power of this work every day. I cannot separate myself from being a coach. I am here to shine a light on the possibilities within others so they can choose to live their most brilliant YES lives for themselves.

Part of the not-so-secret sauce to having what you want is to be honest. So I need to be honest with you.

I am not writing this book because I want to, I am writing this book because the book chose me to be its conduit, and I accepted. I am writing this book because I know that the best things in life come when we honor our commitment over our preferences. While I'd prefer to not write a personal development book, my commitment is to create transformation.

I am committed to you living an extraordinary life, starting right where you are today, with all of the circumstances and history that you have, being exactly who you are. Because who you are is totally enough!

Before we dive in, I'm going to offer a few agreements. If you agree, I invite you to keep reading. If you don't agree, I invite you to put down this book, and move onto something else. I don't need you to be here if you don't want to be here. I love you and celebrate you for following your own heart instead of reading something you "should" read because it will "help you."

The 10 Agreements

1. Let's agree that you don't need to like what I'm saying in order to apply it and get value from it. Some(many) of the things I'm going to share with you might feel crunchy, spicy, stretchy, and just downright uncomfy. You don't have to like them. I'm not writing this book so that you feel warm and fuzzy reading it. (But there are parts that I think will make you feel like that!) I'm writing this book because I fully believe that if you apply what I'm offering, you will get to live your very best life. I care far more about your forever joyful, abundant life than how much you like what I'm saying for the few hours you're reading it.

2. Let's agree that my job is to share what I know, and provide some new possibilities for you to explore; and your job is to try it on, take what's for you and leave what isn't. There is only one expert on your life, and it's you. I will never pretend that I know more about what's in the highest alignment for your life over you. I am here to offer, you get to decide what you take and what you leave.

3. Let's agree that I am a life coach, and for the duration that you are reading this book I am *your* coach. As your coach, my commitment is to your goals, dreams, and fulfillment. My commitment is not to how comfy you feel in each moment.

I am going to say things that call you forward. This is the best way that I can be of highest service to you.

4. Let's agree that you are allowed to have whatever feelings and experiences you have. All feelings are welcome.

5. Let's agree that this is not intended to be a book where I pretend to have all the answers about your life, or that if you just follow the "3 simple steps I took" that magically your life will forever change. That's all just silly marketing speak people use to create a hook. This is a book where I'm going to ask you to do the heavy lifting. You're going to get to search for your truth and make the choices most aligned for you.

6. Let's agree that you have blind spots and I am going to hold up a mirror for you to look at them. There are patterns, beliefs, thoughts, and ways of being that you are unaware of. That's just how it goes for us as humans. Just like you can't always see the car driving next to you on the road because it's in your blind spot and you need a mirror, I am going to hold up a mirror for you to see what's going on in your subconscious. The mirror is here, but you still need to look. Then, make a choice to mind what's in the mirror, or not. I have blind spots too, and I use resources and others to help be my mirrors.

7. Let's agree that this can actually be an incredibly fun, transformative adventure. I know I said I didn't want to write this book, but now I'm a few pages in and getting VERY PUMPED. I cannot wait to hear from you about the way that you've powerfully shown up for yourself and given yourself the life you are worthy of.

8. Let's agree that our goal is not to change you. You are not broken. You do not need to be fixed. You are whole, complete, lovable, worthy, and exactly who and where you are meant to be. Our goal is to have you look at some parts of you that you didn't know to look at and to deepen into a version of you who is ready to be seen.

9. Let's agree that if you ever share this book with anyone as a referral (thank you!) you won't say, "You *should* read this book." Anytime we tell someone what they should do we are contributing to conditioning that perpetuates so many of the obstacles we face. Instead, you could invite them to read it by saying, "I love you so much, I want to invite you to read this book."

10. Let's agree you are willing to really listen, hear, try on, take to heart, and see how it could be possible for you with everything that I share. You don't have to like it, but if you let it apply to you, your life could be changed.

Check in: What inspired you to pick up this book? What is the thing that you've been wanting to say yes to, but money, time, or approval has been a speed bump?

I've been wanting to say yes to _____

I'm going to invite you to make a vow to yourself. What is the promise you feel called to make to yourself right now? It might be to finish this book or actually take on all of the exercises. Or it might be to stay open so you can uncover a new possibility for yourself.

I vow _____

One more thing before we really get into the heart of this book... Why would you even want a life coach, or to make any of these agreements in order to have transformation, anyway?

You are worthy of having all of your dreams and more. Having a coach is a support structure for you to spend less time getting in your own way and more time having what you really want.

As I write this book, I'm thinking about the hundreds of life coaching clients that I've supported over the years and their incredible success stories.

- I think about Carlee, who made $30,000 in six weeks as a photographer before she was even twenty-one.
- Alex, who now is a mom of three, running three businesses, and learning how to make herself a priority.
- Deb, who navigated ending a relationship and choosing to live in her fullness, while running her lucrative business and being there for her team and family.
- Emilie, who retired early, launched the business on her heart, started a podcast, and found joy while also moving through a grieving process.
- I think about Kia who is starting her foundation to make an impact for others while living her dreams as a model.
- I think about Erin who already reached peak financial success, and then took on the heart-work of prioritizing personal development to be the best self for her and everyone around her.
- Christine, who met me $25,000 in debt, as a single mom, terrified to make an investment in herself. And in our first six months of working together made her first six figures as an entrepreneur.
- Chris, who came to us in March of 2020 just as her brick-and-mortar business was shut down with no clue how she would provide for her family. She prioritized standing in her worth and built a record-breaking business being at the top of her industry in her community.
- Kate, who left a job managing a restaurant to open her studio and grew it into two businesses that supported both her and her business partner while on maternity leave.
- Xeres, who trusted herself to follow an unconventional path and found success as an author, healing generations while she walked in her truth.
- Katie, who found the partner she had been looking for and started a relationship based on authenticity and love.

- And Claudia-Sam, who followed her heart to move her and her partner from Canada to New Zealand while continuing to grow her business.
- Robin, who became a best-selling author and lives steadily in her power.
- Nikki, who is running her first half marathon, launched a podcast, and is an amazing mom and entrepreneur.
- Lauren who eloped with her family by her side living out her dream of getting married in the Grand Tetons in Wyoming.

And on, and on, and on.

Whatever YES you are wanting, it's waiting for you. Having a coach is an incredibly valuable tool on your path to financial abundance, rock steady relationships, travel, health and vitality, and deepening your spirituality.

Here in the beginning, I want to tell you that this is just that: the beginning. You taking on the work offered in this book can change your life. Transformation comes from you continuing to choose it.

Consider this book a test drive for having a Life Coach. For the rest of this book, I'm your life coach. Then we can keep the party going.

Are you all in? Head over to Riseleadershipcircle.com/yes for links to our online communities, information about how to keep working together after this, and other resources so that you can get the most out of this experience and connect with others choosing this transformation for themselves too.

Chapter 2

Meet my Mom

Before we go any further there is someone very important for you to meet. You'll call her Lisa, I call her Mom.

Mama Lisa is royalty. Any of our clients will tell you this. She is sunshine. When you are around her the only thing you can feel is compassion, love, strength, and a divine feminine quality that soothes and comforts.

Not only is she my mom and best friend, she's my business partner. Together we run our coaching company, Rise Leadership Circle. Yes, it is the honor of a lifetime.

Our personalities are very different. I am bold, loud, fast, now, go! Lisa is steady, together, patient, divine, receive. We like to say that I am an insta-pot and she is a slow cooker.

This yin and yang is the magic of our work together. We are both highly intuitive and can energetically dance together like a dream. (Side note: We can also tear it up on an actual dance floor. My mom LOVES it when we're at a wedding and I ask the DJ to hop on the mic and dedicate "Get Low" by Lil Jon to her as her favorite song. Read: this is very much NOT her favorite song and she does not like when I do this, but she gets low anyway.)

One of the things my mom has become accustomed to over our life together is me volun-told-ing her for something. This book is no different. My mom absolutely has hundreds of books inside of her that I cannot wait to read every word to. This book, however, I am clear is not one she was thinking she would be writing right now either.

Here is the transcript of me informing her that we would be writing this book. We were on vacation in Savannah. I was doing my makeup in my bedroom, she was doing her makeup in the bathroom.

Loudly, I say so she can hear me from the other room, "You know how sometimes I get these directives from God? Knowings that I just have to follow? With mixed feelings I have to say that I have been directed to write a book that is everything I want to say to someone when they have a dream and are getting in their own way. I don't want to write this but I'm going to. I understand this is a Divine assignment. I'm going to write the entire book in one month. It's all there bursting out of me, I just need to sit down and pour it out. I need you to be involved. I'm going to assign you stories and exercises to include and you're going to have to do it, okay?"

Lisa, *deep sigh* "okay, sounds interesting."

By interesting she means, "I'm both supporting you and looking forward to seeing what you create." And also, "I don't think that's really how writing a book works but I know she's going to do it her way so let's just see how this goes."

If this doesn't give you a peek into what our relationship often looks like I don't know what would.

But we both understood this: the words in this book matter. Not because we are writing them, because you are reading them. You have decided to take a step toward your dream.

Even if we didn't have "write a book" on our plan this year (trust me, we did not), we DID have on our plan to "help a lot of people transform their lives."

This is how Lisa and I work. We flow and braid together. One gets an intuitive nudge and the other one picks up the strand.

While I'll be laying down the foundation of this book, Lisa is going to be contributing stories, exercises, and wisdom that only she can provide.

Keep your eyes peeled for the gold that Lisa weaves in. Take what she offers.

Chapter 3

My Lightning Bolt
Moment of Possibility

The moment that I now think of as my lightning bolt of possibility was unexpected. It felt jarring and fast. I'm going to give you the highlight reel, then we'll go back to share how I got there.

I hit the curb while I was driving into my apartment complex. I was on the phone having a sales conversation with a coach and leadership training program that I so desperately wanted to be a yes for. The investment was $16,500. The program started in three weeks. It required me to travel to a different state and be in-person for the training one weekend a month, every month, for the next year.

At that moment I was more than $100,000 in debt. I did not have a savings account, let alone a spare twenty-dollar bill lying around. I *did* have one credit card with a $500 limit for emergencies. I took out that single life line and put the $500 deposit for the program on it.

I said yes to me. This was an emergency for my soul.

What I learned in that moment was that I am a powerful creator. I learned that I am worthy of my dreams and my circumstances are not my boss. I get to decide what is possible for me. I learned that I can lead with my soul's desire, and then create the resources, support, and spaciousness to bring it to life.

This is an invitation for you to choose you. If you are willing to prioritize your soul's desires and create access to the resources, support, and spaciousness that you need to make your dream manifest, buckle up, we are going for a ride.

***

Now, let's go back to how I got there: in my car, hitting the curb, making a $16,500 investment that on paper I had no business making.

My whole life I told myself that I am bad with money. I believed that I didn't have whatever secret superpower other people had to be able to save or invest money. I learned to be a good discount shopper out of necessity. I liked to shop, and I was on a very slim budget.

It wasn't just that I believed I was bad with money. It was that I didn't think I was worthy of having anything more than I had. I grew up middle class with my parents working hard to give me a good life. I didn't personally know anyone who was easily living in extravagance, and I certainly didn't think that would be in the cards for me.

I both felt like not enough and too much. My self view was that I was very average. Nothing special would be coming my way. I felt not smart enough, not fit enough, not savvy enough, not talented enough. And I was also far too much; too loud, too bossy, too needy, too much work to deal with.

When I thought of my place in the world, I imagined that I would live the rest of my life repeating some version of what I currently had: just enough to get by and occasionally, if I got lucky or worked really hard, a bit of extra indulgence.

I compared myself to others a lot and wanted to be more. I wanted to get excellent grades, be well-liked, and not feel so broke all the time. I put myself under an exorbitant amount of pressure to always be better.

This drive for perfection did not come from my parents, they were always loving and celebratory of exactly who I was. It was completely self-inflicted. At the end of sixth grade our report cards got sent via mail in the summer. I watched our mailbox like a hawk. On the day the report card finally arrived I tore it open to see that I got a "C" in science class. I was devastated, humiliated, and felt like an incredible loser. I locked myself in my room and sobbed.

We had a trip planned to go to a cabin with my dad that weekend (by this time my parents were divorced) and I did not allow myself to partake in any fun. I punished myself for my terrible performance.

Finally, I showed my parents my report card sobbing and apologetic. They were proud of how hard I worked. I didn't understand why *they* didn't realize how terrible getting a "C" was.

The rest of my years in school brought more of the same.

Finally, during my freshman year of college this pattern of demanding perfection from myself and then always coming up short caught up with me. Something had to break, and it turned out that what "broke" was me.

At the age of nineteen I had a stroke.

The stress caught up with me and while a part of me was apparently seeking for a way out, a larger part of me was fighting for a new start.

I am grateful that I made a full recovery. But the piling on of stress didn't stop. I was so conditioned to expect greatness from myself that I just kept pushing.

This was one of the singular most terrifying experiences of my life—for seven months we worked with a team of doctors searching for answers about why I had a stroke and came up empty handed.

After graduating college with a mountain of student loans I took a job in Chicago (let the record show that my mother told me was not the right job for me), rented an apartment I could hopefully afford (I couldn't) and moved to the big city.

In less than a month I was crying, hard, every day before work. My mom came for a visit and on a Monday morning I was laying on the bathroom floor sobbing to her that I could not go another day. This job was killing my soul. I called my boss and quit. There was no two-week notice in this office—a fact I had observed as I watched people quit every day of the month I worked there, never to be seen again. My boss replied, "Nice knowing you, kid" and hung up.

So there I was, living in Chicago with an apartment I could not afford, I had no job, and I still had all that student debt that my payments were about to start on. **Gulp.**

I pieced together a few jobs and was still not making enough to cover my rent, let alone groceries or any other bills. Now I was really feeling like a loser. My anxiety was at an all-time high and I felt worthless.

I found myself back in the hospital. I was having a phantom stroke. My body was in such a state of anxiety, panic, and overwhelm it recreated the symptoms of a stroke.

The medical bills piled again.

A friend moved into my dining room-turned-bedroom and I almost survived a whole year in Chicago. After ten months and enough sleepless nights, I came home.

What I knew about myself up to this point was that I was a quitter. I couldn't hack it, and I should have just stayed where I belonged.

I made some promises to myself after moving home. Those promises were:
- Marry someone who is happy being the breadwinner and will gladly pay for everything.
- Never become a homeowner.
- Live with my mom as long as possible.

Pretty inspiring, right?

I was dating and having exactly the kind of relationships you might expect someone with this attitude toward herself would have. I dated men who were nice enough, but I was never actually happy.

Finally, I got my dream job. This was the job I desperately wanted out of college but didn't yet have enough experience for. Now, three years later I was ready, and they hired me.

I saw a massive bump in my salary. I now made just enough to pay the minimums on all my bills each month and share an apartment with a roommate. My one luxury was a nail appointment every other week. After that, all of my money was spoken for.

For years my mom had been begging me to total up how much debt I actually had. I preferred being in complete denial. I just paid the minimums as they came each month and went about my merry way.

Finally, I caved. I logged into all my accounts and to my shock and horror, I learned that I had more than $100,000 in debt.

I couldn't even wrap my head around how much money that was! I resigned myself to paying off my debt for the rest of my life.

As the months went on the shimmer of my "dream job" wore off and I once again found myself asking for more. There was this relentless voice inside of me who urged me to keep growing.

One cold Saturday night in January I was laying in my bed, I hadn't washed my hair in days, I was feeling depressed that I was once again feeling so unfulfilled, stuck, and out of options. I was eating chocolate while scrolling social media.

Between bites of my chocolate bar, I saw a photo that stopped me in my tracks. There were two entrepreneurs that I knew and respected together at a graduation ceremony for a coach training program.

I had an intuitive knowing like never before: I was being given a clear sign that enrolling in this coach training program was my next move. Years before my mom had gone through a coach training program to help support her team at the business that she owned, so I had a basic understanding of what it meant to be a coach. I had secretly been toying with the idea of either going back to school to get a master's degree, or join a life coach training program. Seeing this photo instantly had me knowing what choice I wanted to make.

I mustered up every ounce of courage I had, which wasn't much, so I knew I had to act fast. I typed in the website of the coach training program and booked a sales call for Monday morning, chocolate bar still in hand.

For the next two days I swam in feelings that I knew well: guilt and shame. I felt foolish for booking this call for a program that I knew I couldn't afford.

I also got even more down on myself for being in this spot that I had been in many times before, so badly wanting something and knowing that I'd have to say no because of my bank account. I was yearning to have my life go differently, but I didn't know how. That glimmer of desire is what had me show up for the call, shame and all.

It was two days later that I found myself hitting the curb while driving into my apartment complex while on the sales call, saying yes to investing $16,500 that I certainly did not have.

That moment was one of those scenes you see in a movie, where you know that nothing is going to be the same after.

When I was getting all of the program information my heart sank. I was hoping she would tell me that the next group started in September following a school schedule and that I could qualify for a student loan. Instead, she told me that the program began in three weeks, I would need to travel out of state for one weekend a month, every month for a year, and that this program wouldn't qualify for a student loan, but I could possibly get a personal loan.

Even with all of the despair I was feeling, there was something new, too: possibility. This still, wise part of me quietly and confidently asked, "What if you said yes?"

I knew that what I *should* do is apologize for wasting her time with the call, but my higher self was asking me to enter new territory.

The land of yes.

It wasn't that I decided to go more into debt, it was that I decided to bet on myself, which until this point had been a rarity. There was that strange feeling of possibility again.

The next day I walked into my credit union and asked for a personal loan. Do you know how bold it is to be a twenty-five-year-old, six figures in debt, having the audacity to ask for more money? It is BOLD, my friends. And I think being willing to be audacious like that is what it takes to really step with our full bodies into our dreams.

They said they'd give me a loan for half of the tuition. I gratefully accepted.

Three weeks later I was headed to my first training weekend. By month six I was still deep in debt, but growing my courage. I got my first paying client! Now I did something really wild: I gave notice to my corporate job.

Yup, I was only halfway through my program, had one paying client, massive debt, and I decided this is when I would walk away from the job that was paying my bills to live my dreams.

I kept fiercely trusting myself, and putting myself in situations where I would need to rise into my greatness instead of melt to circumstances.

My first year as an entrepreneur started with a lot of tears and a roller coaster of doubt and possibility, but it ended with me writing a new six-figure story.

I was now a woman who could receive six figures.

Chapter 4

Let's Get Curious

What dream is calling to you? I am certain that there is something inside that is asking for you to claim it. You wouldn't have been drawn to this book if there wasn't.

Perhaps it is crystal clear, a vision that you play in your head on repeat. Or maybe you have no idea. It could be that you've been feeling stuck, lost, and maybe even numb for so long you don't trust yourself to even know what a dream calling to you would sound like.

Even if we don't know what the dream is, can we agree that one exists? There is a part of you that is being pulled to a deepening or an expansion, and apparently, you've answered the call enough to pick up this book.

This is a perfect place to be. Let's start right where you are. We're going to do a few journal prompts to discover what you are here for.

Note: simply reading the questions and moving on will not create change. Of course, you can choose your own adventure, but it's kind of just like reading the menu at a restaurant and not ordering or eating anything. You're still going to be hungry.

So take on the journal prompts. Write as much as you can. Let it feel silly and strange.

One more thing, I started dancing when I was three and continued to be on a team throughout college. My first and favorite dance teacher, Miss Barb, would always say, "if you feel like a dork, you're doing it right." The same thing applies here.

Journal Questions for Self-Discovery from Lisa

Below you'll find a few of my favorite journal prompts to spark a deeper connection to your dreams. I believe that our big dreams are soul inspired. When we pursue what brings us joy and makes us feel most alive, we're in alignment with our highest self.

Our dreams invite us to become the truest version of who we are because reaching them requires us to release and rewire past limiting beliefs and patterns and to see ourselves as fully worthy, capable, and whole, becoming all that we can be.

Sometimes our soul-aligned dreams don't make perfect logical sense and at first glance they may not seem practical. For this reason, you may have ignored the subtle messages from your soul and instead followed the logical path that others have taken before you.

Journaling can help awaken this connection to your dreams as it guides you to access your inner wisdom. Give yourself as much time as you need and just let your pen flow without filtering your responses.

- What are three things you truly love about yourself, and why?

- Reflect on a recent challenge or setback. How did you respond to it, and what does this reveal about your relationship to yourself?

- Consider a time when you felt most alive and fulfilled. What were you doing, and why did it resonate with you?

- Imagine your ideal life five years from now. What does it look like, and what steps can you take today to move closer to that vision?

- Write a letter to you from your future self—the version of you who is living your dreams and has fully embodied all of the self-confidence, trust and belief you are currently calling in. What does this version of you most want you to know?

Chapter 5

Desires & Dreams

Now that you've started to snuggle up to what is calling you, we're going to identify if this is a dream or a desire.

While these two things—desires and dreams—go together like peanut butter and jelly, they are not the same in my view.

It's helpful to understand how dreams and desires are different so that we can appropriately use them both to move us forward.

At least for the duration of this book, let's agree to use these definitions.

A desire is something that you want to experience in the short term. Having this will likely create temporary change.

A dream is something that you want to experience once and for all. Having this will cause lasting transformation.

For good measure, let's take a step back to look at what comes even before desire, which is what I call a craving. A craving is something that we want and can give to ourselves right now or in the very near future. The joy is momentary.

To really get the distinction of craving vs desire vs dream let's use "time for you" as the example for each of them.

If you were craving time for you, this could look like you wanting to unplug from work for the day to give yourself a few hours of self-care. It would feel great in the hours that you weren't looking at your phone or computer, but out walking in nature instead. However, eventually the satisfaction of having a few hours for yourself would wear off and you'd find yourself craving it, or something else again.

If you are desiring more time for yourself on a consistent basis, this could look like wanting to change your calendar to only take meetings four days per week and have Fridays off. It might take a few weeks or months until you can get everything in place to make this happen, but it's still in the short term. And having an extra day off a week will certainly create impact and change, but it's not necessarily something you'll always have.

However, if there was a special event you needed to attend, you might find yourself working again on a Friday. So even though you made a change, there is a flexibility to our desires. They are not necessarily permanent.

If your dream is to have more time for yourself this could look like hiring a part-time assistant. Someone who can support you for twenty hours per week, helping to take care of all the behind-the-scene activities that you are doing that while important and need to be done, don't need to be done by you.

In order for this dream to become a reality it might take months for you to generate the steady income in your business and find the perfect hire, then onboard them. But once you do, you have transformation. You now have freed up an extra twenty hours per week for you to re-allocate to you. You have built the confidence to expand your team and it's once and for all. Even if this particular assistant doesn't stay with you forever, you will always have someone in that role. Transformation has occurred.

And then there's one more layer, things I like to call "bullshit dreams." Bullshit dreams are things that sound amazing, but actually live so far outside what any part of your brain can comprehend as possibility that you won't take any action on them.

This would be like saying that starting immediately you now only work for thirty minutes per day. You would know that there is just no world where you can snap your fingers and have it happen that way. So, though it might be fun to think about having that much time for you, the dream has tipped the scale and it's not even really a dream.

When it comes to cravings, desires, and dreams, and even bullshit dreams, they all are important.

The more that we allow ourselves to have and act on our cravings and desires, the more we train ourselves to trust that we can act on our dreams.

Bullshit dreams tell us where to look to make a real dream. For example, if I have a bullshit dream to move to a new state tomorrow, it clues me into a real dream of wanting to live in a new state. I can start to explore what's in that dream and play with bringing it to life in the months and years to come.

Here's an example of each craving, desire, dream, and bullshit dream to anchor this in for you. This time I'm going to use the topic of fitness.

Craving = I want to enjoy the sunshine and take a walk today.
Desire = I want to dedicate an hour to myself to move my body each day starting this month.
Dream = I want to run a half-marathon this year.
Bullshit Dream = I want to run a marathon today.

You can see how we can have our cravings immediately; we can create our desires with some, but not significant effort, in a span of days to months; and we can prioritize and work toward our dream that is months to years in the future.

A bullshit dream of being able to run a full marathon today, without training, clues me in that there is a desire to dedicate myself to consistent running practices.

Lastly, I want to point out the sustainability of the joy that comes from each tier.

When I honor my craving to go on a walk today, I'm going to feel great while I'm doing it, and probably for the rest of the day. But it's likely that later today I'll have a different craving to rest, and tomorrow I'll have the craving of moving my body again. Cravings are moments of joy that come and go.

When I give myself my desire of moving my body each day, I will have made a change. I have a new pattern where I prioritize myself, and that will support other areas of my life. I just need to be mindful that a busy season can accidentally sway me back to an old sedentary lifestyle. This is more of something that I do (walk) than an identity that I have.

Upon working for and accomplishing the dream of running a half-marathon my identity transforms. I now see myself as an athlete. I am someone who consistently and reliably prioritizes moving my body. It's predictable that I've also had to upgrade my nutrition, recovery, lifestyle, and schedule to accommodate my training. Reaching my goal creates a transformation. I will always be the person who has completed this.

Let's go through one more example of each craving, desire, dream, and bullshit dream so that you can see the difference before you list out your own for each category.

I'm going to use my client Ally's dream for having a committed relationship.

Craving = Go on a date with someone. She wants to get out of her house, make a connection, and feel seen. Hopefully the date will be great, but a few hours after that joy might fade.

Desire = Be consistently going on dates with the same person. Now she is starting to feel the beginning of a relationship. Life will feel different than when she was single, but it's not necessarily permanent yet.

Dream = Be in a committed relationship with someone she sees a future marrying. This creates transformation. Her life will once and for all be different than how it currently is.

Bullshit Dream = Find her future partner today and get married tomorrow. I'm not saying it's impossible, but the likelihood of her being with her true soulmate in this short of a window is unlikely. However, it does reveal to us what she really wants, which is to be married.

Let's identify your desires and dreams for different areas of life.
You can also identify any cravings/bullshit dreams if it's helpful to make sure that your desires and dreams are in the sweet spot.

Health (consider emotional, physical, or mental)

A craving I have is:

My desire is:

My dream is:

A bullshit dream would be:

Home (consider design, organization, your physical space, how safe and peaceful you feel)

A craving I have is:

My desire is:

My dream is:

A bullshit dream would be:

Money (consider mindset, knowledge, habits, money attraction, wealth creation, and overall relationship with money)

A craving I have is:

My desire is:

My dream is:

A bullshit dream would be:

Purpose (consider your career/work/vocation, creativity, and how much you feel you are actively living your purpose)

A craving I have is:

My desire is:

My dream is:

A bullshit dream would be:

Connection (consider relationships with yourself, loved ones, family, work)

A craving I have is:

My desire is:

My dream is:

A bullshit dream would be:

Faith (consider your personal beliefs, and how you trust yourself and see yourself as worthy)

A craving I have is:

My desire is:

My dream is:

A bullshit dream would be:

Chapter 6

The Enrollment Map

In order for you to get out of your own way and have all of your desires and dreams, it's going to require you to consistently practice one of my favorite things: enrollment.

The definition that I use of enrollment is helping someone get what they want. So, if you're the one trying to get what you want, you need to be enrolled in yourself.

I can't talk about enrollment without talking about sales. Hold the phone—I know, I know, you are wondering why I just mentioned the "S" word.

This is supposed to be a book for personal enrichment, not a business book. Yes, and all personal enrichment leads to sales—stay with me, I'll explain.

Sales are going to have to be involved some way, shape, or form in you getting what you want. Either you will get to make sales through your business or work, and/or you will buy things to help you on your path. Already, you bought this book (sale!).

Sales and enrollment go hand in hand. In order to truly understand what enrollment is, we need to understand what a sale is.

I hear all the time how folks are afraid of being "salesy," or they "don't like being sold." I hear you, and I think that what you really mean is that you are afraid of being seen as slimy or uncaring. Or you don't want to feel pushed into something that isn't in your alignment. I want to invite you to open your mind to embrace a deeper understanding of sales than you may have before, and notice how integral it is to the enrollment process.

We're just talking about sales once in this book, here and now, because I can't separate it from enrollment. I need you to have a basic understanding of how connected these things are so that you can spend the rest of the book getting enrolled in you.

Enrollment = helping someone have what they want.

When enrollment occurs, a sale occurs.

You can't be shy about sales as the consumer or seller if you are gonna get enrolled. And we're gonna get enrolled up in here! (I just felt like I had to write that in a very enthusiastic vernacular, roll with it.)

Consider that there's actually nothing weird or wonky about selling. A sale is simply the moment that a transaction has occurred where party A provides money and party B provides goods or services. That's it. We've gotta stop making sales so deep y'all!

When you go to the grocery store, at the end there is going to be a sale. The cashier doesn't get worried about you thinking that they are "too salesy." They know that you want the groceries that you are buying, and you are prepared to give money in exchange for them.

It's the same if you go to a restaurant. At the end of the meal your server isn't panicked that you're going to be offended when the check comes. Everyone knows that you'll be paying for the meal and service you received.

A sale is just the moment the exchange occurs. A sale was made for this very book you are holding. I promise you I have not been lying awake wondering if any of you are going to think I was "too salesy" for asking you to pay a few dollars in exchange for the wisdom I poured into this book, and the years of experience I took to learn this knowledge.

It can be easy. You wanted to know what I had to say, you wanted to know so much that you were willing to make an exchange with money. Can you feel how neutral that is?

Okay, let's get back to enrollment. Enrollment is helping some-one get what they want. I would say that almost always, at least 99% of the time, for someone to be truly enrolled a sale of some kind is going to take place.

So for you to live a life that you are YES to, and have everything that you want, you are going to get enrolled in you, and you are going to get to sell yourself on the resources to accomplish your dreams.

You can do this, you are worth it.
Make a quick list of 3 things you want to have in your life right now.
1.
2.
3.

Here's my current list of wants:
1. Vegan ice cream
2. A new car
3. Achieve my goal time for my upcoming 5K race

If I get enrolled (AKA get what I want) it will mean that I will end up with these 3 desires. And you would end up with yours.

Let me show you how a sale of some kind would occur for me to be enrolled in all 3 of my current desires.

1. Vegan ice cream - For me to have this, I (or my husband) am going to need to go to the grocery store and buy it. A sale will occur when we take home the ice cream and the cashier takes our money in exchange.
2. A new car - I'm going to get to buy this with real dollars y'all. They just aren't giving away free cars these days.
3. Achieve my goal time for my upcoming 5K race - I get to work with my personal trainer (and pay him money for our sessions.) I also get to invest in new running shoes (the sale will happen at the store). And, I get to run with my friend on the trail we like. It costs me money to put gas in my car to meet her there (another sale at the gas station).

If I'm unwilling to exchange my money for those things, I won't have my desires. So being enrolled (getting what I want) means that I get to be SO enrolled that a sale will occur.

This is going to be true for any desire you or anyone else has. Helping someone get what they want ultimately means that someway, somewhere, a sale is going to be made.

Now, this sale might not be with us, but it will occur. I think it's so helpful to understand that we are enrolling ourselves and others into our desires and dreams all the time. We tend to put more significance (and fear) when the sale will be made with us, but we don't need to.

When we can be committed to enrolling (helping someone get what they want) and neutral about sales (the exchange of money for a good/service) we, and everyone around us, gets to have what they want.

If you are around me, I will be enrolling you in what you want. Why? Because you want it! I am here to help people live their YES lives, which means being a yes to ourselves, our dreams, and our desires.

Enrollment is a willingness to own our desires; to embody our worth so fully that we take action to go from wanting to having.

To help model how often I am enrolling, here is a quick list of enrollments I participated in the last few days.

- I was at Target and asked an employee where the false eyelashes were. She showed me and then we started talking about the magnetic lashes. She said to me, "I'd love to wear them for special occasions but never can get the glue to work." She told me what she wanted, now I'm in enrollment mode. I explained to her how I can never use the glue either, but the magnetic lashes are so easy, you just put on the special liquid eyeliner and the lashes magnet right to it, easy as that! She was so enrolled she said she was going to buy a pair too.
- I was shopping with my mom and she said, "I love this desk. I think it would look great in my office." I took a stand for her to buy the desk.
- I wanted chocolate cake for my birthday. My mom tried making brownies and they didn't turn out. I said, "That's okay, I really wanted chocolate cake anyway." She got to buy a new cake mix and try again.
- My sister wanted sushi for dinner. We went out for sushi.
- My friend told me she wanted to start playing pickleball. I stood for her to sign up for the league near her.
- One of my clients wanted support with making more sales. I enrolled her in joining the Sales Sprint I was hosting the next week.

The list goes on. What are you noticing?

Do you see how I don't have attachment, rather I stand for

people to take action to have what they want? As a result of that, eventually some kind of sale is going to be made.

This is the magic of sales and enrollment. We have what we want and the resources that will give it to us.

Let's get back to you. Remember that quick list of 3 desires I had you jot down a bit ago? What is the sale that will take place as a result of you choosing to have them?

1.

2.

3.

Can you see how if the sale doesn't actually occur, there isn't enrollment? It wouldn't work to go to our favorite restaurant and "be enrolled" in having pasta, but then not order it. Either we're enrolled in getting pasta and we pay for it, or we don't order it and we're not enrolled.

As an act of love, answer this truthfully for yourself, have you ever told yourself, "I'm so committed!" and pretended that you were fully enrolled in having what you wanted, but then when it came time for the sale you didn't actually buy it?

It's sneaky, and a thing we do as humans. We tell ourselves we're enrolled, but we really aren't. That is a disservice to ourselves.

You are worthy of your desires and dreams.

The only way we can stand for others to have what they want is if we are choosing to have what we want. We can't enroll any-body in anything else if we're not enrolled in ourselves first.

Have you ever read a book that started with a map at the beginning? It's a helpful resource so that you can make it real for yourself and connect with where on the map the action is happening.

I have a map for you! It's called the enrollment map. While I'm going to share it with you now, it's probably not going to make much sense until we work through all of the chapters. My recommendation is to dog-ear this page so that you can keep flipping back and see how the enrollment scale, the enrollment steps, and the places we get stopped most line up and impact where you are on the map.

The Enrollment Map

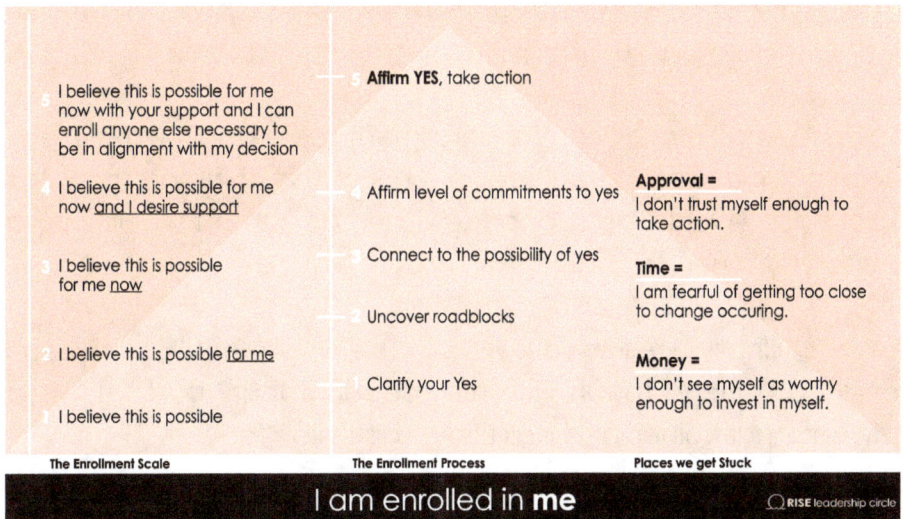

We're going to work through this map together going left to right, bottom to top.

The Enrollment Scale

Level 1- I believe this is possible.

Level 2- I believe this is possible for me.

Level 3- I believe this is possible for me now.

Level 4- I believe this is possible for me now and I desire support.

Level 5- I believe this is possible for me now, with support, and I can enroll myself and anyone else necessary to be in alignment with my decision.

Let's walk through a few examples of where we might get stuck. I'll go first with a real-life example.

Level 1- I realized that I had a dream buried inside of me to run a half-marathon. I've always known it was possible, meaning I knew that *someone* could run a half-marathon, I just wasn't sure that someone could be me.

Level 2- Then I moved up the enrollment scale and decided, yes, it would be possible for me to run a half-marathon, someday.

Level 3- After sitting with that possibility, I moved up again and decided that even now (meaning this very year!) I could run a half-marathon. I could begin training without delay.

Level 4- And I moved up the enrollment scale again when I realized that I was so committed to running this half-marathon, this year, that I would be supported. I decided that I would hire a personal trainer.

Level 5- Finally, I reached level 5 in The Enrollment Scale when I enrolled a friend to run with me (accountability buddy!), hired my personal trainer, and paid the registration fee.

Here is an example of my client Claudia-Sam moving through the levels of enrollment for her dream of living in New Zealand.

Level 1- She knew it was possible to live in New Zealand. There were other people living there.

Level 2- She decided it was possible for her to live in New Zealand.

Level 3- She decided it was possible for her to live in New Zealand now, as soon as all the proper approvals and documentation were in place, which she began the process of securing.

Level 4- She decided she could live in New Zealand now and be supported. She found renters for her current home in Canada. Renting out her home supported her by giving her the resources to rent a new home in New Zealand.

Level 5- She enrolled her partner, her family, her clients, and friends in her decision. Her partner moved with her. Her family made plans to visit. Her clients adjusted their call schedules with her. Friends she had in New Zealand opened up their homes to help her settle in.

When you think about one of your dreams, which level are you getting stuck on in The Enrollment Scale?
Level 1- You're not sure if it's even possible, for anyone.

Level 2- You know it's possible for someone, you're just not sure if it can be possible for you.

Level 3- You know it's possible for you, you're just not sure if it can be possible for you right now.

Level 4- You know it's possible for you right now, you're just not sure if you can access the resources to be supported.

Level 5- You know it's possible for you right now, with resources and support, you're just not sure if you can enroll anyone else necessary to be in alignment with your decision.

Having the awareness of where you are on The Enrollment Scale is supportive, because then we know what to address to clear that block.

Before we wrap up this story, I want to share about a time I worked my way up the enrollment scale. Before I was an entre-preneur, I was working in Corporate America, feeling unfulfilled, at what I once believed was my dream job. I wanted to be an entrepreneur. I knew that I was a visionary with big ideas, and also that I was too bohemian for corporate red tape.

I was at Level 1 belief. I knew that it was possible to be an entrepreneur, millions of other people were, but I didn't know if I could be one of them.

Eventually I moved to Level 2 when I decided that it could be possible for me and (filled with terror and excitement) enrolled in a Coaches and Leadership Training program. (Remember that $16,500 investment I made with money I didn't have?)

Then came Level 3 when two months into the training program I dedicated that I would be leaving my 9-5 before the year was done. It was April, and I told myself that I would let my boss know my intentions by August. I fulfilled my commitment to myself and my last day was at the end of October. I was becoming an entrepreneur now!

I had now arrived at Level 4. I was an entrepreneur; well actually I was unemployed, but intending to be self-employed. And I needed support and resources. I made three more investments that felt big and scary with money I didn't have. I hired a coach, committed to a year membership at a boutique fitness studio, and started a program with a chiropractor. I was setting myself up to be supported personally and professionally.

And then Level 5. I got to enroll anyone else necessary to be in alignment with my dream. I had already enrolled Tom, my now-husband, who was my boyfriend at the time, and the rest of my family in my decision. The people that were left for me to enroll were clients! I got to start building my business while anchoring into my Level 5 belief in myself, thus being fully enrolled in myself and my dreams.

***

Lisa here, I'm going to share a story with you about a time when a dream was placed on my heart and I had to get radically enrolled in myself to follow the path I had been given.

Many years ago, I awoke one night around 3am having a lucid dream. As I opened my eyes, I saw a woman standing in my bedroom doorway. She had really curly hair and looked like a combination of Ms. Frizzle and Amelia Earhart. She was wearing something akin to a 1920s aviator outfit with a leather helmet and goggles. She smiled at me and said three words, "Ready for adventure?"

I sat upright and rubbed the sleep from my eyes. Before logic arrived to explain it as a dream, she was gone, leaving me with the question rolling around in my mind.

In fact, I was ready for adventure, although I had absolutely no idea what that would entail exactly. I just knew that I was feeling stagnant and ready to follow my heart and begin something new.

Now wide awake with little possibility of getting any more sleep for the night, I grabbed my laptop and headed up the stairs to my office so I wouldn't wake anyone.

Somehow, I was immediately guided to a webpage for a school I'd never heard of before, but instantly knew it was exactly what I was looking for. After spending the rest of the night researching and learning about what was offered, I booked a call for the next day.

By the time we got on the call, I knew I was a yes, but when I heard the price of the program, I felt deflated. I had recently paid off some credit cards and was committed to not getting back into debt. I knew I could come up with the money—eventually. I was between level 3 and 4 on the enrollment scale.

I was a soul-level yes, and I knew it was right for me. I knew that I could generate the resources eventually, but I let old patterns resurface and decided to wait.

I remember picking up the phone to call Kaela to tell her I was ready to move in a new direction and take on a new certification. I told her about the 3am dream, the serendipity of being guided straight to this webpage, and the soul-level yes I was feeling.

"There's a new cohort starting next week" (this was January), "but I'm going to wait until April," assuming she'd agree with my logical mind.

"Why are you going to wait?" she asked incredulously.

I explained that I wasn't sure I'd be able to generate the resources so quickly, and of course, she enrolled me back into my own creative power. I decided to have a conversation with my fiancé that night, and we came up with a plan. I enrolled the next day.

If you don't currently have someone supporting you and believing in you, don't let that stop you. Seek out a community and friendships with people who are chasing their own bold dreams, but never hesitate to be your own biggest cheerleader first.

Before asking for advice from anyone, be sure to check in with your own inner knowing above all else and don't seek leadership from anyone who isn't first leading themselves.

Chapter 7

The Enrollment Process, Step 1: Clarify Your Yes

So we know where we want to go: Level 5 enrollment and belief in ourselves. But how do we get there?

The Enrollment Process, of course!

Enrollment is helping someone get what they want, and there is a step-by-step process that guides us to do that.

We're going to move through this process together, but first we have two prerequisites.

Prerequisite 1: Being ready is a decision
Being ready is a decision, not a feeling. Read that again.

If we wait until we feel ready, it's likely that we've missed the boat. I like to say that the best time to leap is just before we're ready.

Ready is not a feeling. We hold ourselves back by waiting for a feeling that doesn't exist. Ready is a decision.

We decide we are willing to move forward, and then we feel however we feel in response. Maybe you feel excited, or maybe you feel nervous. However, you feel is okay. It's helpful to use our feelings as data or information, and to remember that our feelings are what comes between our actions, they are not the key decision makers.

Prerequisite 2: Human Self vs Higher Self
I believe that all of us have "two selves;" our human self, and our higher self.

Our human self is how most of us show up, most of the time, if we are not intentional about being in our higher self. We know we're acting with our human self when we can quickly access things like fear, doubt, and using logic to override intuition. Think of wearing a lot of layers and filters that you view the world through when you are in your human self.

Our higher self is free from conditioning and filters. This is when we are in direct connection with our Source and love. It's the part of us that is connected with possibilities and trust. We can connect with our intuition and use logic to support it.

As we move through the rest of the process, notice if you are coming from your human self or higher self. Remember, it's not good/bad, right/wrong to be in one or the other, but it is helpful to notice which self is driving.

Okay, back to our regularly scheduled programming...

The Enrollment Process, Step 1: Clarify Your Yes

If we are going to enroll ourselves into something, we first have to be crystal clear with exactly what that thing is.

What are you wanting right now? What desire or dream is calling to you?

Let's clarify your yes. What specifically are you a yes for?
Start with "I am a yes for..." this might be something like
- Leaving my current job
- Starting a new relationship
- Signing up to run a 10k
- Enrolling in a photography course
- Hiring a life coach
- Booking a vacation to Spain

Each of my examples are tangible and specific, I'm not including how having that desire will leave me feeling, yet.

Once you know what you are a yes for, let's clarify it by identifying what you are a no for. I know this might seem obvious, but naming what you are a no for is very supportive in the enrollment process.

Here are a few examples of no's that correlate with my example yeses above.
- Staying in my current job
- Staying single
- Continuing to work out just when I feel like it
- Treating photography like a hobby instead of a career
- Having desires and not taking action
- Wishing I could travel and feeling envious of others who do

Keeping your yes in mind, what specifically are you a no for?
Now that we know that, we're going to clarify your yes even more.

What's important about you having this desire or dream?
Answer this question for yourself with as much detail as you can. We're asserting that your dream matters, this is your chance to fight for it.

What makes "now" be the right time for you to bring this desire or dream to life?
How come you feel so called to this dream now? What do you know is different about you than a previous version of you? Why do you feel you need to go for this now instead of waiting?

Who else will be impacted by you having this desire or dream?
You also might consider how they imagine they will be impacted and how you see they will be impacted.

I work with a lot of female entrepreneurs who are wanting to invest in themselves and work with a coach to grow personally, which will also help to grow their business.

When I ask this question of who else will be impacted, sometimes they'll say, "My kids and my husband. If I'm growing in the way I want to I won't be such a people pleaser, always taking care of everyone else's needs first. And if I'm growing my business, I will be working more and not always home to make dinner or have the time to do all the extra things I do for everyone."

When I ask how their family might feel about that their initial response is something like, "It would be a tough adjustment for them. They really depend on me and they won't like it if I'm not always available."

And of course, everyone gets to feel however they decide to feel.

I continue, "How do you see that they'll be impacted?" They respond, "They'll get to take on more responsibilities. They can practice becoming independent and creating what they need too. They also get to watch me have my dream, and they would be proud and supportive of that."

Listen, y'all, I have to ask you this directly—if someone is not rooting for every ounce of your success, are they really *for* you?

If there is someone in your life who would rather that you stay small, dim your light, compromise, sacrifice, or bide your time in service of their personal preference or comfort there is something to look at.

I'm not saying drop them like a hot pan. But it is time to hold up the mirror. You having desires, and then having those desires come true is never a problem. Someone in your life telling you that you can't have those desires, or that they'd prefer you don't so they can be comfortable, *is* a problem.

But here's the good news, once you have the awareness that's what happening, you can get to work on it. Rather than sitting with a problem, you have the opportunity to grow your relationship so that both partners get to have their desires come true. Now instead of a problem, you have a gift.

How will you feel when you have this desire or dream?
Feelings are information, not decision makers. And as information they are valuable guiding lights. When we feel into what it will be like to have our dream and we feel paralyzed, terrified, and in disbelief, that is giving us information that we likely need to refine our dream.

And if we feel into what it will be like to have our dream and we feel expansive, excited, and energized it's giving us the green light that our higher self is onboard.

The first step in moving up the enrollment scale from Level 1: I believe it's possible to Level 2: I believe it's possible for me, is to be clear what we are actually a yes and a no for.

Chapter 8

The Enrollment Process, Step 2: Uncover Roadblocks

Now that we've completed Step 1 you are crystal clear on exactly what you are a yes to your desire or dream, including:
- What are you a no for?
- What's important about you having this desire or dream?
- What makes "now" be the right time for you to bring this desire or dream to life?
- Who else will be impacted by you having this desire or dream?
- How will you feel when you have this desire or dream?

So now you have already moved through Level 2 "I believe it's possible for me." We're going to keep climbing the enrollment scale to Level 3: I believe it's possible for me, now.

Step 2 in The Enrollment Process is to uncover roadblocks. Here, we are looking for any and every speed bump that could slow us down, or a roadblock that could stop us on the way to creating our dream.

We're looking for circumstances, limiting beliefs, old patterns, and situations that are predictable.

Start by simply asking this question,
What are any speed bumps or roadblocks that might slow you down or get in your way?

Go ahead and start making a list of anything that comes up. Be sure to consider the following:
- Circumstances (any conditions that are occurring)
- Limiting beliefs (something you are holding as true that may or may not be)
- Old patterns (a way you've always done something)
- Predictable situations (based on how you know yourself or others to act)

Let me share with you a non-exhaustive list of some of the most common that I hear…

Circumstances:
- Age
- Being in school
- Working full-time
- Status of bank account
- Amount of debt accumulated
- Capacity on calendar
- Having children
- Planning for an event coming up
- Holiday coming up
- Summer
- Slow season
- Being single
- Being married
- Taxes due soon
- Awaiting/recently received a big bill
- Purchasing a house/car
- Physical body shape/fitness level

Limiting beliefs:
- I can't afford it
- I am too busy
- It's not the right time
- My partner doesn't support me
- I need to do it on my own
- I haven't earned it
- I'm not experienced enough
- I need to wait
- I need to complete my certification first
- I have to pay off a bill first
- I'm overweight
- It hasn't worked before

Old patterns:
- Waiting
- Stalling
- Delaying
- Overthinking
- Overanalyzing
- Checking with partner/friend/accountant/financial advisor/children
- Trying to do it alone
- Rushing in
- Low self-belief

Predictable situations:
- I won't follow through
- I'll give up
- I won't tune in
- It will be hard and I'll get frustrated
- Nothing will change
- Someone else will need something
- We'll get a surprise bill

And the number one thing that I hear most often when I ask, "What are any speed bumps or roadblocks that might slow you down or get in your way?" is...

"Me. I get in my own way."

That, my friends, is the most truthful of all the answers.

Here's the deal, everyone has circumstances, limiting beliefs, old patterns, and predictable situations (I call that being a human :)) The difference is in being the kind of person that sees those as obstacles, or as opportunities.

I subscribe to the belief that we are given "problems" so that we have the opportunity to have the solution.

In my experience, the people that actually get what they want are the ones willing to be truthful about all of their speed bumps. And the biggest speed bump typically identified is the one about how they have been acting like a saboteur.

And the people that say, "Speed bumps? Oh, I have none! I know exactly what I'm going to do. It's all figured out. I just need to do it," are the ones who stall out the longest spinning their wheels.

This is why: when we bring all our possible speed bumps into the light, we are informed with all of the solutions (AKA powerful ways of being) we're going to need to keep moving. When we pretend that there will be absolutely nothing that could possibly slow us down even a tiny bit, we are playing ourselves and it's most predictable that we'll get stopped fast and have no resources for how it can go differently.

I need to be clear on something. None of these speed bumps or roadblocks are actual problems. They aren't evidence of you being broken, and they certainly aren't information about why getting what you want won't work.

While you may want to say they are your reality (and I'm not here to argue) I'm also going to call it like I see it: they are simply circumstances, limiting beliefs, old patterns, and predictable situations. I am not diminishing them, or telling you how to feel about them. Remember, you get to feel however you decide to feel. But the circumstances themselves, they are neutral, what's so, or what's happened in the past. They mean nothing about who we are and what's possible for us other than the meaning that we give them.

Consider that if a bee stings you (circumstance, something that happened) it doesn't mean that you're not worthy. It means that you got stung by a bee. And getting stung by a bee doesn't mean anything about you. Even though this is a very "light" example of a circumstance, neutrality holds for all circumstances.

At this stage, we aren't looking for any solutions or other possibilities, we simply want to name all our roadblocks so we won't be surprised when they come knocking.

What are any speed bumps or roadblocks that might slow you down or get in your way?

Chapter 9

The Enrollment Process, Step 3: Connect to the Possibility of YES

Once we know what you want, and the most predictable things to slow you down we get to add my favorite ingredient: magic.

I already know some of you are groaning and eye rolling, "I have real bills, Kaela. My life truly is hectic. Magic isn't going to do anything."

Slow your roll my friends, we've gotta trust the process, okay? Stay with me for a few minutes. Remember, if you always do what you've done, you'll always get what you've got.

When's the last time you tried magic? Okay then...

We are going to pretend that we can magically move all of your speed bumps and roadblocks out of the way.

We are NOT going to consider HOW these things clear out of our path, we are just going to use your imagination for a few minutes to pretend that they are.

Lock into your imagination…3…2…1…blastoff…

You know what you want. All of the speedbumps and roadblocks that you once had have been magically cleared. You can walk right over to your dream and claim it.

Go ahead, imagine yourself living your dream. Your desires are alive. This is your reality. Stay in that place and answer this next very important question…

Now what's possible?
What is possible beyond your dream? As a result of having your dream, what else opens up?

Keep your imagination rolling here. If your dream is to live in a house on a few acres of land with animals you love, picture yourself there.

Now what's possible? Do you start hosting retreats? Do you open up a farm stand and provide produce and animal love to your neighbors?

Do you build another building on your land and start renting it out, creating another stream of income?

Or maybe your dream is to find your partner and get married. So there you are, a few months into wedded bliss. Now what's possible? Are you starting a new job? Are you planning to grow your family? Are you taking the leap to leave your corporate gig that feels like a j-o-b and finally open the bakery you've talked about for years?

Perhaps your dream is to have a few rental properties so that you can live from the monthly recurring revenue. Imagine opening up your bank account on the first and seeing that everyone paid rent for the month. All of your bills are paid and there is a surplus.

What's possible now? Are you starting a course to help others create this for themselves? Are you getting ready to travel abroad for six months? Are you planning to foster a dog and spend your days making pasta from scratch, reading a book by your fireplace at night?

Live your fantasy.

When you snuggle up to what's possible beyond your dream, do you feel expansive? Does it call to you? Do you see that version of your life and know, "this is meant for me?"

Great. You did it. You officially used magic to pretend and for a few minutes to interrupt the part of your brain that is addicted to knowing how. This was a success, friend.

We get to connect to this yes, to this possibility. Are you willing to be a yes to your dream, in service of stepping on the path to *this* bigger dream? If so, we keep rolling.

Sometimes the reason we say no to our dreams is because they aren't big enough. We're sneaky like this. If the thing we think we really want isn't really going to make that much of a difference in our life we might think, "why bother?" So much effort for a little reward, even if it's what we want.

When we see what else is beyond our dream, when we tap into the next level we are called higher. We are using a deeper vision of what's possible for us to encourage us to choose our dreams.

But remember, we have to choose it.

Here's a tip from Lisa on how to anchor into this possibility to keep it close:
Your dreams already exist—as energy. Think about this—everything that exists was first an idea, a thought, a possibility before it became a thing.

This book, for example, existed as an idea until Kaela brought it to life. The chair you're likely sitting on? Yep, it existed as a design in someone's mind, until they took the steps to turn it into what it is today. Think about our smartphones, who could have imagined that one day we'd be able to run an entire business simply from the phone in our hand? Someone did—and now we all rely on it as part of our everyday lives. Everything starts in our imagination first.

Your dream functions exactly the same way. Give yourself permission to dream as big as you can, as often as you can. Spend time daydreaming. Write about what you imagine your life to be when your dream is now your reality. Let it fill you with possibility and excitement.

Visualizing your dream daily will strengthen your belief (much like a daily workout will build muscle) and anchor you into deeper levels of possibility and expansion.

Chapter 10

The Enrollment Process, Step 4: Affirm Level of Commitment to Yes

By this point our excitement is growing. We are feeling deeply connected to what we want, and even though we might not know how, we know that we are called to our dream and we are craving it.

So we're going to check in and make sure that were A) being truthful with ourselves, and B) getting courageous with ourselves. The next step is to ask ourselves this key question, "On a scale of 1-10 how committed am I to having my dreams, now?"

1 = It sounds cool but I will take no action.
10 = I am fully committed. I will take action even if I have disempowering circumstances, even if I have to invest time, money, and energy. Even if I don't know how.

This is where we find out if we've been playing ourselves.

Most people answer 8-9. OR, they say 10, but they mean 8-9. A few say 10 and mean it. Those are the ones that quickly experience their dream coming to life.

To me, an 8-9 says, "I really WANT this dream. But I am hung up on the how. I cannot figure out how I would commit if I don't know how."

And 10 say, "I'm willing to lead with courage. I'm willing to have this go differently. I'm willing to commit and let that be the first step in the how revealing itself to me."

Please hear me: Whatever truthful answer you give to this question is perfect. You get to be right where you are. Maybe you are not at a 10. You may not be willing to have this dream exist yet. That's okay. Being truthful with yourself is helpful because now we know that we can go back and pick up a different dream that you are willing to be a 10 for.

This is your life. There is no need to "should" yourself into anything.

If you are a 10, truly, this is where we buckle in.

Being a 10 means that we are willing to surrender. We are willing to walk a new path where we do not try to figure out the how. Instead, we stay open to the how revealing itself to us one step at a time.

The first step is being willing, all in, fully committed. We don't know any more than that. We activate courage.

When we are a 10, we'll know because we will affirm our commitment with immediate action. This means we make a bold move that brings us closer to our dream coming true. Let's walk through a few examples.

If your dream is to find your partner and you are committed at a 10, you might take action to sign up for a dating app, or sign up for the co-ed pickleball league you've been thinking about.

If your desire is to heal your gut and become the healthiest version of you, the action that you take might be hiring a dietician and health coach, or you might order the book you got recommended to you.

If your dream is to grow your business, getting new clients this year, the action that you might take is joining a mastermind or signing up to attend a conference where your ideal client might be.

As you can see, whatever action you take corresponds to your desire or dream. And, there is something in common with all the actions: they will require investing time and money.

It will take time out of our day to go on a date, attend pickleball, meet with a health coach, read a book, tune in for a mastermind call, or go to a conference.

All of them will require some kind of financial investment too. This is how we know that we've taken an action bold enough to get us moving towards our dream: there was a time AND financial investment involved.

Loving Interruption: *Consider that any action that is only one or the other, time or money, isn't the kind of action we take when we're committed at a 10. So either it's a way that we are sabotaging ourselves, or it's revealing to us that we're not yet committed at a 10.*

This is the place where we have a check and balance system for ourselves. If we are committed at a 10,, we'll take a bold action that involves both time and money. And if we're willing to take that action it means we're committed at a 10.

But what if you're not there yet? That's A-okay. We start by being truthful. If you are 6 or less, we're going to do ourselves a favor and start this process over with a different dream, one that we're willing to be committed to.

If we are committed at a 7-9, we're going to play with our curiosity. A great question to ask yourself is, "What's between my current level of commitment and being committed at a 10?"

Some common things that come up are:
- I would be committed if I had a plan
- I don't have the money to invest in making it happen yet
- I'm so busy right now
- I'm afraid of how life will look if I go for this
- I don't know that it can happen for me

Recognize any of these things? The objections that we're used to using in order to defend our limiting beliefs are sneaky and sticky.

This is a moment where we give ourselves compassion and grace. And we then ask this follow up question, "Even if I don't know how, am I willing to take the actions to bring this dream to life?"

If yes, we keep going. If not, then we know that this is where we are. We've come up against the biggest roadblock: willingness.

It's okay to not be willing. What I need you to know is that when we are willing, we will; when we are not willing, we won't.

You get to decide. If you are truly not willing, the most compassionate thing that you can do for yourself is own that decision. And when you think about this dream instead of believing a lie that "It can't happen," say a more loving truth, "I am not choosing this right now."

You can always change your mind, or not. We get down on ourselves when we believe the lie that our dream can't or won't happen.

Being truthful and owning that we are not choosing it to happen right now gives us all the power. We remind ourselves that it is our life and we get to choose. If you are truly unwilling, let yourself be unwilling. Own that as the spot you are for right now. Explore another dream that you are willing to bring to life.

Chapter 11

The Enrollment Process, Step 5: Affirm YES, Take Action

In Step 4 we identified the action to take; now we're going to take action! And there's a very important key about this action: it needs to be immediate.

We don't delay, or think about it, or tell ourselves that we're going to do it later. We get on it.

We take out our phones and download the dating app, or click the link for the pickleball league and submit the form with payment. If we are hiring a health coach we get online and submit an inquiry form to talk to the person that we want to work with. If we're starting with a book, we order it online right away.

Or we pay for the mastermind or secure the conference tickets.

Visit riseleadershipcircle.com/yes to take action to work with us inside our coaching containers.

We don't put it on our calendar to do it later, we take action right now. Taking action means taking action. One of the greatest gifts that you can give yourself is the gift of follow through. This is where you are creating a new habit, and trust in yourself, that you can show up for yourself.

What's the action that you're going to take right now? _____
_____

Go take that action.

Chapter 12

Places We Get Stuck

You might be reading all of this, better yet, moving through these exercises in real time, but maybe you're running into a little snag.

There might be a part of you that is trying hard to pump the breaks with something I like to call an objection.

Just for fun (because if we're not having fun, what are we even doing?) let's imagine that we are in a courtroom and your soul just slayed in outlining why you, the defendant, should absolutely have your dream.

It seems like this is a closed case, you're ready for the judge to pick up the gavel and grant you access to everything you've been wanting.

All of a sudden the plaintiff, the human part of you, yells "Objection!"

Can you relate? Have you ever felt so close to having what you want and then your human self barges with an objection?

I have good news for you: objections are a positive thing. An objection means that your human self knows shit is about to go down and is pulling out all of the stops to keep that change from happening.

An objection simply means there is a part of us that is looking for information to feel good about the choice it knows that our soul, or higher self, has already made.

We don't have objections to things that we are certain aren't happening.

Have you ever been to a mall with little kiosks in the middle? There's always a sales person offering things like, "try our hair straightener." I'm guessing that you don't stop and tell them all the reasons why you're not going to stop and straighten your hair if you have no desire to straighten your hair.

You'll likely just smile and say, "No thank you," as you walk on by. No objections. If there wasn't any part of you that wanted to get your hair straightened, you're not going to have any objections.

But if the place you were walking to in the mall was Macy's because you are on the hunt for a new pair of boots, and you find the perfect ones, it's far more likely that this is where you'll start to have an objection.

If the boots you love cost more than you were hoping they would, or if you were thinking you were going to get a black pair, and now you're really wanting both black and brown, this is where the objections come into play.

And the reason for the objection is because there is a part of you that has already decided this is what you want. You've fallen in love with the boots, and the price tag is higher than you intended, the objection is saying, "I know that I want these, how can this happen?"

Objections come up when we want to be a yes. If this happens for you, welcome it! See this as an opportunity to grow through a limiting belief or old pattern that keeps you at a distance from having what you really want.

There are three objections that as humans we most commonly bump up against. They are:
- Money
- Time
- Approval

Money objections sound like, "I don't have the money." "It's not in my budget." "I can't afford it." "That's too expensive." "I need to save more first." "I have too much debt."

Time objections sound like, "I don't have enough time." "I'm too busy." "My schedule is maxed." "I'm overwhelmed as it is." "It's not a good time." "I need to wait until X is finished."

Approval objections sound like, "I'll have to talk to my spouse." "I need to see what my financial planner says." "I need to see how much I owe on taxes this year." "If I get as much back on my taxes as I'm expecting, I can." "I'm just waiting to get my schedule, if it's open I can go."

How many of those do you find are in your typical repertoire of objections? If you are like most people, probably most, if not all of them.

While objections are a positive thing because it means that we're working out how we can actually have what we want, they are also the place where we stop ourselves most.

This is the corner of sabotage and circumstance. The way most people live is by having their circumstances create objections. Then, people around them accept those circumstance-based-objections as facts that cannot be changed.

Moving through life like that doesn't help anyone, especially you.

I'm not saying that your circumstances aren't real, I'm saying that they don't have to stop you. Objections can either be a chasm or a catalyst.

If we treat our circumstances-turn-objections as chasms that's where we stop. It's the end of the road for our dream.

When we treat them as catalysts, we get to use our circumstances as reasons why we get to have our dream. And that, my friend, is powerful.

Ready to live your YES life? Let's lift ourselves through our objections into our dreams.

Chapter 13

Places We Get Stuck: Money

I need you to know that money objections typically aren't actually about money. We like to think they are, because it takes fear of looking inside of ourselves and not liking what we see and puts the blame on something outside of us.

The good news is that even if we look inside and don't like the patterns of realities we see, there is no need for blame.

I'm not saying that if you told me you didn't have the money in your bank account for something that you want that you'd be lying. I would believe you, but I wouldn't believe that's the reason that you can't have what you want.

Our bank accounts are not our bosses. They're not our parents, ministers, town council, or any other authority we've ever looked to for approval.

Our bank accounts work for us, at least they are supposed to. But some of us have got it twisted.

If money objections aren't actually about money, what are they about? Our connection to our worth.

Say what? I know, curveball. Let's break it down.

Side note: For a minute, I'm going to pour my own beliefs all over you. I'm going to ask you to try them on and see how they fit. If you want to take them home with you, cool. If you decide to leave them after this, you do you, boo.

I believe that every human is born infinitely and innately worthy. Period. We don't have to do anything to earn or prove our worth. In fact, we can't. There is nothing we can do, say, believe, to make us more worthy than someone else or than a previous version of ourselves. And there's no way to lose our worthiness too.

But that doesn't mean that we are always connected to our worth. Some of us have been trained/conditioned/learned in a moment of survival to tuck our worth away on a shelf and forget it exists. Or we take it for a spin on a special occasion, but treat it like a fur coat we wear to church on Christmas instead of sneakers that go everywhere with us.

We are worthy, but we don't always stand in that worth. Sometimes we'll say that we logically know that we are worthy, yet we still feel like we have to earn or prove it.

Being connected to our worth means that we marinate in it. We stand in it unapologetically. It's not just that we know our worth is unconditional, we embody that knowing.

Question: Why would someone who is disconnected go through all the trouble of accessing money to pay for something they don't really believe they deserve?
Answer: They don't. Instead they say, "I can't afford it."

This way instead of having to look at how they don't feel worthy of their desire (ouch) they can shrug that pain outside of themselves.

Pawning the decision making onto our bank accounts has us feeling a "bummer" when we *think* we can't afford something, but that is less pain than the sting of not feeling worthy.

It hurts to think that we don't deserve what we want. And it hurts even more to believe that we don't deserve it because who we are isn't enough (or is too much), or whatever flavor of that Kool-Aid we drank, so we don't.

We just say, "I don't have the money."

Then sometimes we go right on feeling angry that our bank account is empty (how dare it!) and that displaced anger also feels better than coming to terms with the way we've been feeling about ourselves. (Ouch again.)

Question: What about someone who is deeply connected to their worth, and doesn't have the funds in their bank account for what they want?
Answer: They'll create access to the funds.

Someone who is wholly connected to their worthiness and what's possible for them won't be stopped by a circumstance like a barren bank account. They'll know that their bank account doesn't mean anything about them, who they are as a person.

They'll open up to the possibilities of how they can create access to the money. Things like: making money from providing a service or product, leveraging money on a credit card or loan, borrowing the money from their own savings account or investment fund, asking for the money as a gift from someone they know, receiving the money from a scholarship or grant, etc.

As of 2022 there was approximately 2.26 trillion dollars in circulation in the United States. Someone who is deeply connected to their worth knows that even if the money they need for the thing they want isn't in their bank account, it exists. And it's just a matter of deciding and acting to come into connection with that money.

If we want to be able to afford more things the solution isn't just to make more money, but first to take on the inner work of connecting with our worthiness.

This is crucial so that we activate our money magnet. We have to see ourselves as people who are deserving of money. To do that, we have to see ourselves as deserving. Full stop.

Let's begin.

Chapter 14

A Quick Guide on Connecting to Your Worth

I'm going to introduce you to a graphic that came to me in what I call a "Divine Download." Sometimes God just shows me an image, or drops a concept in my head that I didn't "think" up, but was given to me to share. As soon as I got this download it clicked, and as I've been sharing it with my clients it's helped make what can feel abstract feel tangible instead.

The picture on the next page is a depiction of an iceberg that shows the depth between Dream, Discipline, and Deserve.

We've been talking about what your dreams are. They sit up on top of the iceberg, the vision of what you are creating for yourself. We already know that our dreams consist of desires. Every time we are a yes to a desire, we are flexing that muscle so that we know how to be a yes to our dreams.

Discipline is part of this equation too. Discipline is honoring our commitments. We need to be disciplined to both honor our

The Depth between Dream, Discipline, and Deserve

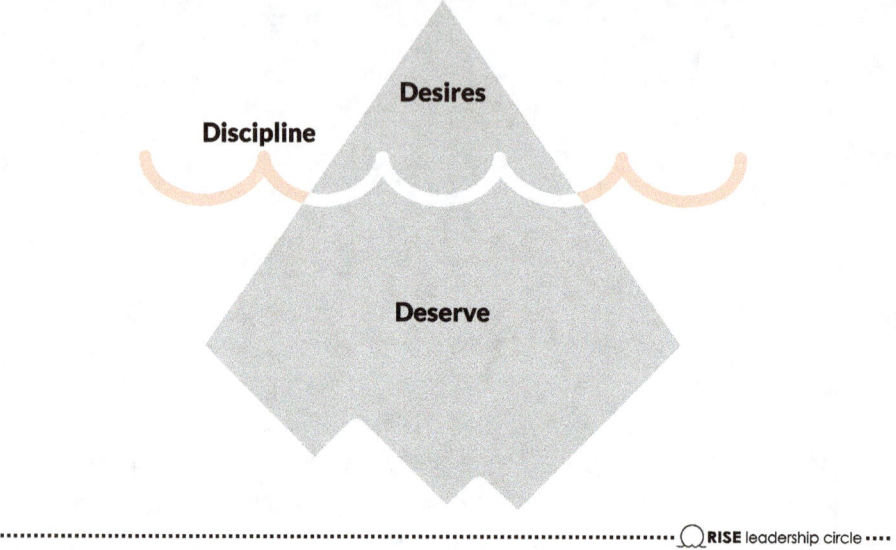

RISE leadership circle

desires and dreams. These three things: discipline, desires, and dreams all work together and exist because of the other.

We get to have our dreams as a result of being disciplined with our desires.

We are disciplined so that we have our desires and dreams.

Our desires open the door for our dreams, and are accessible because of discipline.

Underneath the water is 'deserve.' We can't see it, but it has the most weight. The way that we relate to ourselves and what we deserve, or think that we're worthy of will determine how disciplined we are with our dreams and desires.

If we are not disciplined, or we are not giving ourselves our desires and dreams, the root cause is that we're disconnected from our deserve-ability.

The depth between our dreams and our worth matters. The bigger our dream, the further down we have to sink into our connection with what we deserve.

A little connection with what we think we deserve will result in a little discipline for our dreams.

The more you want to be a yes to, the more you need to own that you deserve it.

So now that you know the first "what" of being able to create access to the funds to invest for your dreams: connect with your worth, let's get into a "how."

In a few more paragraphs I'm about to drop a list of thirty-three ways to connect with your worth so you can fulfill your desires. Here's what all of those things have in common...

We are wanting to explore your beingness, the essence of who you are at the core. Not your thoughts, feelings, opinions, talents, strengths, but who you ARE.

You are worthy because you are. Your worth has nothing to do with anything we can measure, track, grow, or change. Your worth comes from the soul that lives inside your beautiful human body.

The list of ways to connect with your worth I'm going to share below are certainly not the only ways to do this, just helpful practices I've loved using for myself and my clients have taken on over the years.

It's important that you don't view these things as a checklist. Your goal is not to try and hurry through the full list and then wait for a magical moment of connection to your worth.

The intention is to build practices that consistently remind you of the worthiness that already exists and your ability to plug into it.

There's an analogy that I like to use with my life coaching clients when we notice that what's going on is that they've disconnected from their worth. Imagine that you are in a dark room stumbling around trying to find the light switch. Once you do you turn it on and you can see what's always been there. The electricity was running the whole time, you were just unplugged from it.

Then maybe a few hours later you notice that somehow the lights got turned off again. Still, the electricity is running, there's just been a disconnect. Your worth is the same. It's always the same, but sometimes we realize we accidentally had our switch turned off so we can't see the light.

The goal is not to turn on the light in the room one time and never need to flip the switch again. The goal is to know where the light switch is and how to simply give it a flick when we need to plug back in.

This is what taking on consistent practices to connect to your worth does, it's your way of flipping the light switch.

Read through this list of practices. Commit to at least one. If you just go through the motions it won't work. You've gotta take on this practice with heart. Remember, this is about connecting to your beingness deep inside, and getting vulnerable with yourself.

33 ways to connect with your worth so you can fulfill your desires:

1. Look at yourself in the mirror. Speak one thing that is valuable about the person that you are.

2. Find a baby picture of yourself (or imagine yourself as a baby) write down all of the qualities you came into this world with.

3. Recall a time when you were proud of yourself. Reflect on the way of being you had in that moment. Acknowledge that you still have access to that way of being.

4. Think about a pet you have/had. Imagine what it is about you that they loved (not what you did for them, but who you were for them).

5. Write your obituary. This is a very powerful exercise. On the top write "to be used in the year 2XXX" fill in for the year you'll be 110.

6. Call 10 friends up and say, "I have a strange question to ask, I'm doing an exercise from my Life Coach. What are your favorite qualities about me?"

7. Imagine that you were sitting in a white room, completely empty of furniture, etc. There you are sitting in the middle with nothing to do, nowhere to go, no one who needs you to cater to them. Describe the person sitting there.

8. Recall a time when something didn't go as planned. Reflect on the qualities you evoked that allowed you to persevere.

9. Go on a compliment rampage. Open up a page in your journal and write down as many compliments about yourself that you can.

10. Think about the qualities you admire in someone else. Acknowledge that you can only appreciate those qualities because they are alive in you too.

11. Do you have a relationship with God/Creator/Love? Consider that they didn't make a mistake when creating you.

12. Pretend you are a work of art. Write a review for a fictional art show.

13. Reverse psychology: for a short while unintentionally dis-connect from your worth. Skip the shower, eat junk food, watch mind numbing T.V. Notice how eventually there is a part of you that wants something different for yourself. That's the part of you that can never forget how worthy you are.

14. Plan a party for yourself.

15. Ask someone else to plan a party for you. Fully receive.

16. Make a list of your desires. After each one write, "I am worthy of this." Believe it.

17. Make a list of 10 reasons why you should have something your soul is craving. It's okay if all 10 reasons are "Because I am worthy."

18. Do something that brings you joy. Let that feeling all the way in.

19. Ask a relative what they remember loving about you when you were born.

20. Visit the Humane Society website for your community. Look at the page for one of the animals there. Reflect on how you just know this animal is worthy of a good life. Con-sider how you are too. Make a donation on the website.

21. Bonus points! Visit the Humane Society in real life. Cuddle a cat or walk a dog. Verbally speak aloud why they are worthy of a good life. Know you are saying this for both of you. Make a donation before you go.

22. Bake a cake. Every time you add an ingredient, pretend that the ingredient you're adding is something about you that you love. Eat the cake in pleasure.

23. Wake up and say, "Today I'm going to make every choice rooted in my worth." Follow through.

24. Wear your seatbelt and drive the speed limit. Think about how precious your life and the life of every person you pass on the street is.

25. Get in nature. Notice what qualities you have in common with all of the things you see around you.

26. Move your body. Notice how good you feel after. Your body is thanking you for affirming its worth. 27. Sit in prayer or meditation. Empty your mind and notice how your worthiness cannot leave you.

28. Sing a song you like, loudly. This is just for fun. You're connecting with you being worthy enough to have fun.

29. Write a letter to your past self thanking them for specific ways they showed up for you and got you here.

30. Imagine you're a future version of yourself. Write a letter to the now-you thanking you for how you are showing up right now.

31. Reflect on a time in your life that you may regret or wish that you acted differently. Forgive yourself. People who are connected to their worth can forgive themselves. People who are willing to forgive themselves get to know the joy of being anchored in their worth.

32. Go for it! You know that thing that seems crazy, wild, impossible, or like a pipe dream. Take the first action to start bringing it to life.

33. Give yourself a hug.

Which practice will you start with? What would happen if you committed to one of these each day for a month?

There are two more important things that I need to share with you about connecting with your worth.

The first one is that it's not a thing to "do," it's a way to "be." You can't do worthiness, you can simply be worthy. If you're trying to "figure out how" you're working too hard. Worthiness is about unlearning, deconditioning, and dropping the behaviors you took on to show up in a certain way.

At its core, worthiness is about being exactly who you are. The fullness of you. Consider that what can make it feel hard is that it's actually not hard at all. We are conditioned to so much doing, but being worthy doesn't require any of that.

The second important thing I want to tell you is that I want to invite you to have grace for yourself. As you start taking on this practice a lot of feelings might come up.

Let them. It is 100% okay to feel any way that you feel. There may be anger, shame, guilt, or grief about times in the past when you were disconnected from your worth. You are allowed to feel any way that you want. And, you can give yourself grace and compassion.

The previous version of you was doing the best they could with what they had. That's not a cop out or an excuse, it's the truth. We always act with the highest level of consciousness available to us at the moment.

And I'd say that younger you did a damn good job. You got here.

In case there is anything coming up, I want to share a practice from Mama Lisa that might become your new favorite tool. This is her recipe for how to process an emotion.

How to Process an Emotion and Open up Emotional Intel
- Start simple: Just be in the present moment.
- Tune in to your body.
- Notice the physical sensation of the emotion and where in your body you're experiencing it.
- Notice that we generally experience emotions within our chakra energy centers, or the center of our body from our seat up to the crown of our head.
- Typically we don't say I feel this emotion in my left toe, etc. Usually we feel things more in the gut, chest, shoulders, back, head.

- Which chakra or chakras are involved? If you are unsure, that's okay too.
- Focus your attention on the sensation. Notice if it has a shape, a color, feels heavy or light. Draw a picture of it if it helps, or journal what it feels like.
- Just allow it to be.
- Ask the emotion what it wants you to know. Listen, journal if needed.
- Now send the breath to the area where the emotion is being felt.
- On the exhale see and feel any tension or tightness leaving with the breath.
- Exhale, let go.
- Notice when the stuck energy begins to loosen or move— this is what we want—energy in motion.
- Once it begins to move, you'll feel the intensity release.
- It could dissolve completely, or just lessen. Either experience is fine.
- It could take 30 seconds, 2 minutes or an hour. It's all fine.
- You could practice this in one minute intervals if you have resistance.
- Trust your own process.

Chapter 15

Money Trauma

Now that you are someone who is practicing being all up in your worthiness, I want to introduce you to another one of my favorite tools. This is called your Wealth Code.

If you are wanting to create access to money, the fastest, easiest path is by being in your alignment.

One of the ways we block money is by trying to make money or be in a relationship with money with someone else's recipe.

The way we make money is not one size fits all. But we may have been led to believe it has. Have you ever read a book, listened to a podcast, or watched your parents/someone you admired growing up and saw their behaviors about money and tried to copy/paste them to yourself? Only to find that it didn't seem to work as well, and now you're eating a shame sandwich telling yourself you're a loser who's not good with money?

I'm raising my hand. This was definitely my experience.

Before we uncover your Wealth Code, I'm going to spill the tea on some of my own money trauma.

The first time I can remember really thinking about money in a serious way was sophomore year of high school. We had to take a mandatory class called Personal & Financial Management. One of the assignments was for the month of March we were to keep track of every dollar that we spent, or was spent on us. The idea was to get a sense of how much it costs for us to live, so we'd also have a sense of what kind of income we needed to make.

Perhaps a good idea in theory, but let me tell you, not so much in practice.

March happens to be my birthday month, my sweet sixteen no less. It was also prom, the month I traveled as a member of the dance team to Florida to compete in a National Dance competition, and this month I was going back to Florida for a twelve day vacation for my mom's wedding.

Y'all, that might have been the most expensive month of my life!

The kinds of things that were being bought for me for my sweet sixteen birthday, prom, and two trips to Florida, one being a wedding did not come with an itty bitty price tag!

I dutifully carried out the assignment to the best of my ability. At the end of the month the teacher was walking around looking at our spreadsheets. When he got to me he said, "that is a disgusting amount of money to be spent on anyone."

I was mortified. Shame, guilt, and fear flooded in. What I know now is that my teacher was projecting his own feelings onto me. But at sixteen I didn't know that.

I took his comment and internalized it. I made it mean that A) I was unworthy, and B) that money and I are not friends.

I carried on the next ten years telling myself on almost a daily basis that, "I'm bad with money."

When I graduated from college and moved to Chicago, I realized in short order that I couldn't pay my bills without help. My parents chipped in covering some basics and I took on a roommate who moved into my dining room. I retold myself again and again, "I am bad with money."

In my twenties I lived paycheck to paycheck, paying all the minimums on my bills and scrounging away enough for a nail appointment and dinner out with friends. I told myself, "I am bad with money."

My mom urged me again and again to tally my debt from student loans and medical bills. I was in massive resistance. What's the point? It's likely a higher number than I can even wrap my head around. I'll just surrender to knowing that I'm going to be paying it off for the rest of my life. One day I finally caved and totaled it all. It was north of $100,000. I was numb. It almost didn't even matter to me because I believed that number would only grow and that I would never be someone who is debt free.

This tracked with the story that I made up about myself in high school, "I am expensive and I should feel shame."

I can remember standing at the gas pump with $20 trying to decide how much I could put in my tank to make it to meet my friend and still have enough for dinner. "I am bad with money."

I looked around at others who seemed to have a lot more financial freedom than I had, which really wasn't hard since I was scraping by, and I compared myself to them.

I felt immense guilt at how I was with money. I wanted it to be different, but I couldn't bring myself to have it go any other way.

One year for Christmas my mom got me the book of a well-known financial guru. I never even opened the book. I used it as a door-stop before eventually donating it. Just having the book made me feel like a loser. I was someone who was in so much debt, and clearly unwilling to change, because I felt hopeless.

I had known that the premise of the book was to live as lean as you possibly can and use any extra money to pay down your highest debt first, then rolling that money into your next debt.

In theory, I understood that this made sense. I knew others who did this and was happy for them. But when I thought about choosing that for myself it felt so off.

I had been believing that there was one right way to "do money" and I was nowhere near it. I was embarrassed, lost, and resigned to "be bad at money" for the rest of my life.

Until I wasn't. Until I started getting coached and transforming my beliefs. Until I realized that the things I had been telling myself about me and money weren't facts but disempowering stories. Until I opened up my mind to a new relationship with money.

Until I discovered my Wealth Code.

And then everything changed. Let's do it for you, too.

Chapter 16

Discovering Your Wealth Code

Let's start with the definition of financial freedom. While I believe this can mean a lot of things to a lot of people, there is one definition I hear most often: having no debt and being able to pay for what I want, when I want.

Listen, if that's your definition, cool.

But it's not mine. My definition of financial freedom is to be free to make the choices that I want to make, when I want to make them, and to be able to create access to money to pay for all of those things because I say so.

To me, financial freedom is a mindset, not a bank status.

I personally do not feel financially free if I want to do something and my bank account says "No ma'am." I feel restricted, trapped, and like I am employed by my bank account. *Shivers with disgust*.

I feel free when I can make any choice I like, and then create the resources to pay for said choice. This does not have to mean I just go into debt. My solution for everything is not to put it on a credit card or take out a loan, but sometimes that is the temporary next step.

Financial freedom is saying, "I can make that money."

Being able to do that is true freedom. To me at least.

And sometimes the fastest way for me to have something is to leverage money from another resource. If I am committed to having something before I am scheduled to pay myself, next I might put it on my credit card with a commitment to pay it off in a certain amount of days. Your girl feels no kind of shame borrowing money from American Express for a limited amount of time to get what I want, make the money to pay it off before I get charged interest, and rack up those airline points. Thank you very much.

(In fact, I'm reading my final proof read of this book before it goes to my editor while sitting in First Class on a fully-paid-for-with-points Delta flight to New York. Current-Kaela is getting to fly in style for free thanks to my airline points from purchases past-Kaela made and paid for leveraging money on my credit card. I pay my balance monthly to avoid interest.)

In our early 30s my husband and I suddenly found our dream lake house. We weren't looking for a house, just land that we could build a house on years down the road. We had a nice cushy savings built up to pay for a piece of land on the water, but we hadn't yet saved the full amount to build the house.

Our dream house suddenly appeared on the market exactly in the location I was looking for land. We got to leverage money. We were able to put down a sizable down payment, but still had to take out a mortgage that made my jaw drop. (If only my Personal & Financial Management teacher could see my bills now, HA!)

I wasn't willing to sit on the sidelines and let this dream house pass me by because I didn't currently have every single dollar in my bank account. And, I don't feel that having a mortgage means that I'm not financially free. Au contraire, I am free to make any choice I like, and create the finances to back it up.

My husband (AKA the domestic drill sergeant I love and live with) put us on a strict plan to pay off the mortgage on the lake house in twelve years instead of thirty. If y'all knew the kind of interest we were set to pay on this thirty-year mortgage you would be signing up for this twelve-year plan too. More financial freedom. I am free to agree to Tom's intense pay back plan and tell my finances to go to work there.

I personally would not have felt that I was living a life of financial freedom if I saved that same amount of money for the next twelve years to buy the house in cash. I would have felt like I was missing out on twelve incredible years of living my dream life on the lake. To me, having zero debt isn't financial freedom.

Now, maybe you're thinking, "but Kaela, wouldn't you rather have millions upon millions so you could still buy whatever you want without debt?"

Sure, baby! Sign me up. And, I can be financially free now on my way there. Financial freedom is a mindset, not a bank status.

I'm able to see all of this because of my Wealth Code. And if you're getting sweaty palms and feeling nervous for me reading this, it just means that we have different Wealth Codes, which is perfect. Remember, we don't all have to have the same relationship with money—we just get to honor OUR relationship with money.

Your Wealth Code is your unique recipe that reflects YOUR relationship with money (because it's really your relationship with YOU.)

To give you an analogy of how Wealth Codes work, I want to talk about spaghetti for a minute. :)

I think that most of us could agree that a delicious marinara sauce has tomatoes, garlic, onions, basil, salt, pepper, oregano, and if you're from where I'm from: cinnamon.

I could give all of us those same eight ingredients and say "Go make marinara!"

We would all use the same ingredients, but we would likely all prioritize how we use the ingredients differently.

Some people would be slowly roasting tomatoes for hours saying that's the best way to get the most flavor.

Some people would be making sure they have freshly picked basil.

Some people would be prioritizing the salt, making sure it's Icelandic, or Himalayan, or whatever they love most.

I would be making sure to use cinnamon, and some of you would have that last on your list of priorities using the smallest amount.

We can see that while we can agree on what the ingredients are to make a delicious marinara, the way we prioritize them are all different. And each recipe is perfect.

This is the same with the ways that you prioritize the energies within your Wealth Code! It's your recipe, your code for how to be your most aligned self.

You do not need to change it or try to have it be anything different than what it is.

You can also totally love other marinaras and keep your recipe the same. You can at times play with another ingredient as the main focus once in a while, but you'll always hold your recipe sacred.

That's what we're doing. Your restaurant is successful because of your recipe. When you follow the recipe, you win. When you try to abandon it for what you think is right, you experience disharmony.

I'm offering the eight energies listed below as a mirror to show us what alignment with ourselves looks like. The relationship that we have with ourselves informs our relationship with money.

Rather than having respect, admiration, and joy for the unique relationships we can all have with ourselves and thus money, our society has asked us to see one relationship as "right" and "good."

And if not society, it could have been the relationship or pattern that we learned at home growing up or being in a relationship with our partner.

This is an opportunity to make none of it wrong. To allow for it all.

The gift in playing with these eight energies is to see that if we can be in our alignment, we can experience our greatest success. Anytime we are trying to "should" ourselves into anything different we move into misalignment, and that often shows up in our bank accounts.

Our relationship with ourselves and money can be rooted in love, and look different.

Consider that what creates the most financial freedom and alignment with wealth is when we are honoring our Wealth Code, not trying to force ourselves to fit into someone else's.

Let's discover your Wealth Code!

Order the eight energies (below in alphabetical order) from highest priority to lowest FOR YOU. There is no wrong way to do this, except for ordering them in the way that you think you "should." Let your intuition guide you.

- Accomplishment
- Celebration
- Connection
- Generosity
- Pleasure
- Possibility
- Respect
- Transformation

1. _____
2. _____
3. _____
4. _____
5. _____
6. _____
7. _____
8. _____

Okay fam, you've got your Wealth Code! We'll pay special attention to the top three and the last one. I'll tell you all about how to use it in the next chapter.

Chapter 17

Understanding Your Wealth Code

Now you know what a Wealth Code is, and what *your* Wealth Code is, but what does it mean?

Your Wealth Code means whatever meaning you give it. This tool is intended to be a resource that supports you to feel empowered around money. I invite you to create an interpretation of your Wealth Code that feels the most empowering to you. Even if you and someone else have similar or the same Wealth Codes, what that code means can be different for each of you.

I know that it can be helpful to have a guiding light for what to consider when we think about the different ingredients that make up our Wealth Code.

While all 8 energies (ingredients) are part of your Wealth Code, it can be helpful to focus on the top three and the one you ordered last for the most insight.

The energies that you listed as your top three priorities are the things that you care about the most and likely consider when making your decision. The energy that you listed as priority eight might be something that you tend to avoid or not think about as much. We'll talk more about this in the next chapter, but for now consider that all 8 energies are important, and if there are any that we are avoiding we won't be experiencing harmony.

To understand your Wealth Code, it's helpful to understand each of the specific energies, and that each of these energies can have a high expression and a low expression.

The high expression is when we are leaning into that energy in an empowering way that creates balance and harmony with the other energies, and creates alignment and expansion for us.

The low expression is when we are squeezing the juice out of the energy and leaning in so hard it actually becomes disempowering. This creates an imbalance, disharmony, and doesn't leave room for any of the other energies.

Here are places to consider how the high expression and low expression of each of the eight energies in your Wealth Code may be showing up.

Accomplishment

High Expression – Creation energy. You can spot an opportunity and create a solution. CEO mentality, let's keep lifting and growing. Embrace consistent evolution. You are someone who can drive the team towards a goal. Trust that money is continuously coming because you are someone who is a creator.

Low Expression – Always feeling like you need more, something needs to be better or fixed. Nothing is good enough. Hyper drive, losing site of the human components being fixated on numbers or results. Worried about where the next money is coming from if you are in the ebb of just finishing a project.

If this energy is one of the top three in your Wealth Code – Own the CEO that you are. Relish in your ability to create. Be mindful that you are creating space for celebrating and allowing for things to be how they are in the moment. Creating from a space of joy rather than judgment. Practice honoring the journey of both the ebbs and flows.

If this energy is last in your Wealth Code – Consider when a driving energy may serve you. Know that you don't have to be in resistance to motivation even though you aren't led by it. Allow for bursts of creation.

Practices – Connect with a goal that you currently have. Imagine that goal has already been fulfilled, and dream up what your next goal would be. Spend time envisioning what your life will be like when you are playing for this goal.

Make an investment in YOU that feels stretchy. Celebrate how you can do this with ease because of all of the ways that you've created financial security already.

Celebration

High Expression – Energy of winning. Victorious. In the spotlight. Everything is working out. Willing to let others see me living my best life. Life is good now and it's going to be good later. Visibility. Trust that when I use money to celebrate who I am, how I'm feeling, and what I'm creating more will be on its way to me.

Low Expression – Spend to seem happier than you are. Need others to see you so they think a certain way about you. Spend as an impulse instead of connected to a place of celebration. Lose sight of your truth and alignment and become consumed with your image to others. Can spend all of your reserves now rather than allowing yourself to save and invest for the long game.

If this energy is one of the top three in your Wealth Code – Embrace that you GET to celebrate and don't need to put any judgment on it. Let yourself be visible as the empowered person you are. Allow yourself to be fully you, witnessed, and have a relationship with money that comes from this space. Practice honoring your truth rather than focusing on your image.

If this energy is last in your Wealth Code – Consider any judgements or fears that you have about being visible and seen as wealthy and powerful. Is there an opportunity for you to allow for celebration instead of restricting or operating from a space of rigidity in a particular area of your life?

Practices – Share about a recent win with an open heart. Can you allow others to celebrate with you?

Play with creating freedom in a way that feels expansive to you. Consider both short term and long-term freedom.

Connection

High Expression – Relationships are extremely important. Deeply getting to know someone and be for them. Human to human is important to you. Abundance is experienced in who you are with and how you can be in joy together. Money becomes a way to deepen relationships and strengthen connections. Money can be an energy exchange, the icing on a cake for a mutually beneficial relationship.

Low Expression – Prioritize connections so much that money is very much an afterthought or in resistance. Often willing to have someone else handle all things financially. Can let yourself be taken care of by others in a way that's codependent. Ignore finances so as to not disrupt a relationship. Can find yourself over discounting, giving, or not collecting on payment owed because of a relationship.

If this energy is in the top three of your Wealth Code – Honor connections and strengthen them by seeing how money can be a resource. Empower money as a tool to create more and deeper connections. Look at where you can be in a harmonious relationship with money as a connector rather than a disruptor. Practice being in the know with your money like you are with the people in your life. Have a relationship with money.

If this energy is last in your Wealth Code – Explore how creating deeper connections can enhance your potential for wealth. Are there opportunities to create even more abundance because of the connections you make and strengthen?

Practices – Make a list of three people you've recently started a relationship with. Consider how your gifts could be of service to them.

Find out "what's so" with your money. Find out how much is coming in and how much is going out.

Generosity

High Expression – You love being able to give your time, money, ideas, and share resources. You delight in seeing how you can collaborate to create win-win situations with others. For you, people having more, is the goal. You feel aligned when you are in the flow of giving and receiving. You know that you open up to abundance by being generous.

Low Expression – You may find that you give to others more than you give to yourself, or you are great at giving but restrict how much you allow yourself to receive. Be aware if you are experiencing scarcity because of an imbalance of giving/ receiving. Also watch if you are giving in order to prove yourself, be good enough, or be liked. It can be common to have out-standing money owed to you when you're in the Low Expression energy of generosity.

If this energy is in the top three of your Wealth Code – Let your-self be guided by your innate desire to give. Open up to the flow that is activated by your giving. Go ahead and be generous in all of the ways you wish, including with yourself. Remember that when you give to yourself, you will be more resourced in the ways that you can give to others. Pay just as much attention to receiv-ing as you do to giving. They work in tandem.

If this energy is last in your Wealth Code – Play with what could open up for you when you are generous to both yourself and others with your time, money, ideas, love, and resources. Consider that even in the small, subtle ways you share you are accessing another avenue for abundance, one that you don't need to resist for fear of lack.

Practices – Allow yourself to receive from someone else. You may have to make a request, let yourself ask for what you'd like and stay open to it coming to you.

Are you more generous with your time or money? Explore what it would be like if you shifted to be generous with the other for a while.

Pleasure

High Expression – You love to indulge and live in the present moment. It feels good to know that you can delight in your soul's cravings. You live for the yes. There is a high that comes from having a desire and honoring it. When you choose to honor your aligned yes you are living in flow with abundance and wealth.

Having joy in this moment leads you to create more joy in the next. You affirm your worth.

Low Expression – You may find that you give yourself things just because you can, not because you really want them. You can go on autopilot of buying because of the knowledge that you like to receive. Notice if you resist saving or investing for fear that it means you can't have another desire in the short term. Also notice if you are giving yourself things in order to feel loved or worthy.

If this energy is in the top three of your Wealth Code – Treat yourself to that which is aligned. Your work is to affirm your worthiness, love, and enoughness because of who you are and then make aligned choices from that place. Celebrate that when you are feeling good you create more and notice that there is no need to make yourself wrong for it, this is your gift! Play with creating pleasure both from decisions that you make for the present moment and long term. When you are saving or investing for the future consider how much joy that creates too.

If this energy is last in your Wealth Code – Notice any places that you restrict yourself from joy in the present moment. Be curious with how you can both honor your higher priorities while also delighting in the extra yeses your soul is nudging you too. This is an invitation to be spontaneous when it serves you.

Practices – Create a luxurious experience for yourself to pay bills. Consider starting with an Epsom salt bath, pouring a glass of tea or wine, and lighting some candles. Make bill paying a joyful time.

Visualize yourself ten, twenty-five, or fifty years from now having immense financial security. Connect with how pleasurable that feels. Take one tangible action toward that.

Possibility

High Expression – You are present to opportunities coming in all shapes and sizes. You are willing to take a risk because you're connected to the potential result and experience. You operate from a sense of trust and are rooted in resilience. You are often an early adapter and willing to jump before knowing all of the information because you can leap from the plane and sew your parachute on the way down. You know how to create your own soft landing. You have bounce and a commitment to recreation.

Low Expression – You may find that you spread yourself thin being a yes to every possibility that could pay off. You might experience needing to really search for the silver lining to justify a past choice rather than taking the learning. You may be moving at a pace that is too fast to sustain. Also watch that you aren't always flying solo for fear that others in your life won't understand or try to hold you back. Being vulnerable while trusting in yourself is an asset.

If this energy is in the top three of your Wealth Code – Celebrate the trust that you have for yourself. Have an ongoing practice of being connected to your deep desires so that you are making choices to honor them rather than just being a yes because a potential reward exists. Play with the amount of time that you give yourself between having an idea and diving in.

If this energy is last in your Wealth Code – Notice any ways that you resist making a choice that could really serve you because you don't have all of the information. Consider the question, "what would have to be true for me to trust myself at this moment." Watch that you connect with your power coming from your source and within you rather than external evidence.

Practices – Reflect on a time when you made a courageous choice and it worked out. Consider sharing your goals with your partner, notice the power in being vulnerable.

Respect

High Expression – You love having security, stability, and plans for the future. You respect yourself by respecting your resources which includes money. You cherish what you have and use it to the fullest rather than trading it in early or having multiples. You can be savvy and find a way to enjoy nice things and experiences by waiting or doing research to find out how to create the most savings. You are in the know with money; where it's coming from, where it's going, and often live a cash-positive lifestyle preferring to buy only when you can pay in full rather than having debt.

Low Expression – You may find that you judge others who don't have the same commitment to security and long-term investments like you do. You may make choices from the energy of being frugal or from scarcity. Also notice if you are living so much for the future that you are missing out on joy in the present. Are you keeping yourself from dreaming because you don't yet see the pathway for how that could happen with your current resources? Or do you let yourself dream but only with a time frame that is distant?

If this energy is in the top three of your Wealth Code – Stand in the stability that you create for yourself, your family, and your company. Know that you often may be the rock in relationships because of your natural ability to play the long game. Stay open to ways that you can experience security and joy in the present moment simultaneously. Allow yourself to embrace spontaneity and big dreams because you are rooted in saving, investing, and having a plan for the future.

If this energy is last in your Wealth Code – Notice where you are resisting looking at long term goals for fear of not being able to enjoy what you want now. Explore how you can respect yourself because you have a dynamic relationship with money where you allow it to stay in your life instead of just immediately using it.

Also play with really being in the know with what is going on with your money.

Practices – Buy something at full price.

Play with embracing a bigger vision. Dream a bigger dream than you've let yourself before.

Transformation

High Expression – You are an out-of-the-box thinker who can transcend current structures. You have the gift of alchemy—taking a base thought and amplifying it into a new result. Relationships and emotions are likely important to you and you have a perspective of the world that may seem different than the status quo. You are here to revolutionize and create new ways of operating, including with money. You likely create access to money in non-traditional ways. You likely really stand by your morals and beliefs.

Low Expression energy – You can feel defensive over your beliefs and get into a binary right/wrong way of seeing things. You may feel confronted by society's request to track achievements and ways of measuring success and wealth. Consider if you find yourself completely at odds with money and the belief structure that would have created that. There also may be a lot of judgment toward current systems, people who operate within those systems, and even yourself at times for operating or not operating in those systems.

If this energy is in your top three – Know that marching to your own beat is your gift. You do not need to confirm, and you can be in a space of allowing and acceptance which creates harmony in your life. Play with the ways you can have a relationship with money that feels peaceful and powerful, knowing that it may look different than how others experience money.

If this energy is last in your Wealth Code – Play with what possibilities exist if you expand beyond your current relationship with money to one that has no rules or limits. Consider opening up to other perspectives and views including around money and the systems money operates in.

Practices – Consider a change that you want to see. Explore how money could be a resource to aid with this change.

Practice unhooking from judgment. Notice how judgment creates resistance. What is possible when you are in an energy of flow?

Check in:
When you consider the descriptions of the high and low expressions of each energy offered here, what comes up for you?

_____
_____
_____

Which energies have you been operating with the high expression?

_____
_____
_____

Which energies have you been operating with the low expression?

_____
_____
_____

What would be possible for you by practicing being in the high expression of each energy in your top three, and bottom energy more often?

_____
_____
_____

Chapter 18

Honoring Your Wealth Code

Now that you have an understanding of your Wealth Code, it's time to practice honoring it. *Practice* is a way to expand rather than force. When practicing something it doesn't mean that you lock yourself into the high expression of each of the top three energies of your Wealth Code, never to waver. No, it is an invitation to play.

Practicing means you explore and notice what it's like to be in the high and low expression of each of the energies in all sorts of situations. There is no right or wrong way to do this. Practicing is an invitation to use your Wealth Code as a resource that creates an experience of empowerment and alignment.

Specifically, making decisions keeping in mind, and embodying, the high expression of your top 3 energies in your Wealth Code, and also being aware of your last one (instead of ignoring it) is what will create alignment and power.

This may mean that you choose to think about things, or make choices differently than those around you, differently than people you love, differently than what you've seen in society, differently than how you were raised, and even differently than what you've done before.

Without the knowledge of our Wealth Code, it's likely that we'll hold beliefs and make choices around money that come from conditioning. Conditioning is what we think we "should" do, because it's "best" or "right."

Our Wealth Codes invite us to be in relationship with money in the way that is most aligned, free from should/best/right. What is most aligned for you in your Wealth Code may look different than others.

Let's use this as a space to play with honoring your Wealth Code in different scenarios.

Reconnect with the high expression of the top 3 energies in your Wealth Code, then let's apply them to what I call "The Big 6."

The Big 6 Ways to Be in Relationship with Money
    Attract
    Save
    Invest
    Spend
    Give
    Honor (commitment to sources where you leveraged money; debt)

Attract is when you call in money to flow to your bank account. You might think of this like "making money," "generating money," or "earning money."

I personally prefer to think of this as attracting, meaning to receive money. Feel free to think of this concept in whatever way speaks most to you.

When you are in the high expression of the top 3 energies of your Wealth Code, what is the most aligned way for you to attract money?

_____

_____

_____

Saving money is when we set it aside for a short to medium period of time. We save money with an intended purpose to use in the coming months or years. Most savings accounts don't offer a significant amount of interest to be paid on money sitting there, so we want to think of a savings account like a holding zone for money we will be using in the near future.

For example, you might be saving money to buy a car, or to cover a program you're going to join, or for a vacation fund.

Pro tip: It's a great idea to have an emergency savings fund that has enough to cover 3 months of expenses. I recommend finding a financial institution that offers a high interest rate on the funds in that account. This way you'll still have fast and easy access to the money, and you'll be earning interest while that money sits there.

When you are in the high expression of the top 3 energies of your Wealth Code, what comes up when you think about the most aligned way to save money?

_____

_____

_____

Investing money is when we send our money somewhere to generate a greater return in the months and years to come. We can think of this like long term savings, but instead of keeping the money in our regular bank accounts, we put it somewhere specific to help it grow.

We can invest money by putting it into investment accounts. This is a way that money can work for you by growing over time. You may want to work with a Certified Financial Planner or do a deep dive and research which options are most aligned for you.

Another way to invest money is by using it to pay for a training or development program. For example, if someone invested money in college to become a nurse, in the years to come they would end up receiving far more money from their nursing salary than they would have if they just kept that tuition money in their savings account.

We can also invest in personal development, like working with a coach, which supports us to grow as a human. The more that we grow, the more that we open up to even deeper aligned ways of attracting money. The return on investment of arming yourself with support and resources to grow personally is high.

I want to share a quick story about my client Chris. I first met Chris in March of 2020. We connected the week that businesses had needed to close down due to the pandemic. She was making all of her income from her brick-and-mortar massage business and was fearful about what this would mean for her and her family.

She decided to trust herself with the investment in joining our coaching program, even though money was scarce in her bank account, and there was no certainty of when or how it would be created.

She invested in herself. We worked on both the inner work of Chris the human, and also the tangible ways to grow her business. Chris has continued to work with us for the last four years. She has created more than six figures of revenue in her business the last three years. Investing in her personal development yielded a high financial return for her and her family.

Consider the possibilities of investing both with investment accounts, and development opportunities.

When you are in the high expression of the top 3 energies of your Wealth Code, what comes up when you think about the most aligned way to invest money?

_____

_____

_____

Spending is how we use money day-to-day and short term. We spend money on things like groceries, bills, shopping, weekend getaways, etc.

Spending money allows our basic needs to be met, and also gives us an opportunity to be a yes to the things that are most joyful for us.

It's up to you if you consider things like a mortgage payment, an investment or a monthly expense. I personally see it as an investment, though I know that it can feel like an expense. You decide how to categorize things like that in the way that is most empowering for you.

When you are in the high expression of the top 3 energies of your Wealth Code, what comes up when you think about the most aligned way to spend money?

_____

_____

_____

Giving money is when we send our money to bless someone else with no intention or need to receive something back from wherever we are sending it.

There are a lot of ways that we can give. Consider that if we are getting something in exchange, we are spending the money. If we are sending the money with no strings attached, we are giving it.

We can give money to nonprofits, people we personally know who could use our support, people we meet who ask for our financial help, etc.

When you are in the high expression of the top 3 energies of your Wealth Code, what comes up when you think about the most aligned way to give money?

_____

_____

_____

Honor (commitment to sources where you leveraged money; debt).

Honoring previous commitments to sources where you leveraged money are things like loans, credit cards, or any payment plans that you made for services/products previously received with money to be collected on an ongoing basis over time.

Aka debt. Now hold up a second. I want to invite you to shift your possible perspective around debt. I want to remind you that things only have the meaning we give them. You can decide to have any relationship and boundaries that you want with debt. And since you get to decide, why not decide to have it be an empowered relationship?

Many people tend to view debt as something to have guilt or shame over. Another possibility is that you can choose to see it as making an agreement that you now get to honor. Is there shame in honoring an agreement? I don't see it.

When you are in the high expression of the top 3 energies of your Wealth Code, what comes up when you think about the most aligned way to honor previous commitments with (debt) money?

_____

_____

_____

How does it feel to have some new places to play? Is there more space for creativity, possibility, and expansion?

Can you see a new belief that you get to try on or a new pattern to explore? Perhaps you can even tap into a new identity as someone who is worthy and abundant.

Chapter 19

Making Money is an Inside Job

By now you're starting to get a sense of a paradigm that transformed my life: making money is an inside job.

Before (when I was broke, unfulfilled, and felt like a big-time loser and victim to my circumstances) I thought that the way to make money was to work hard, earn it, and prove how worthy and valuable I am.

By now I think you can tell I certainly don't subscribe to that belief any more. I actually can't. I now have *way* too much evidence to the contrary.

What I have seen made real so many times in my own life and the lives of my clients is that making money is an inside job. Think back to a few chapters earlier when we talked about a disconnect from our worthiness as being the foundation of a money roadblock.

If an "inside" thing like our connection to our worthiness is what keeps us from accessing money, it would make sense that inner work is the path to money.

While I also have seen instances of people muscling their way to money, I know that it's not fulfilling or sustainable. Becoming a match for money from the inside out is both.

What's the inner work to take on to be a match for money? Well, the recipe can look different for everyone, and there are a few key ingredients:
- Embodying your innate worth
- Embracing your Wealth Code
- Leading with joy

We've already covered the first two, now let's get to leading with joy.

Another belief I hold (because I can't not—again I have too much evidence to support this truth) is that money follows joy.

Everything is energy, and energy is everything. That's all money really is: energy. As energy, it can be attracted and repelled.

Here's a list of the top money repellents:
Shame, guilt, apathy, grief, fear, desperation, need, want, anger, pride.

Here's a list of the top money attractors:
Courage, neutrality, willingness, acceptance, reason, love, joy, gratitude, peace, enlightenment. Think this is all woo woo mumbo jumbo? I'm coming in hot with science.

All of the repellents and attractors I just listed are emotions and states of being. Scientists measure them using a unit called Hertz. The frequency of the top money repellents ranges from shame at 20 Hz to pride at 175 Hz. The money attractors range from courage at 200 Hz to Peace at 600 Hz, and Enlightenment at 700-1000 Hz.

Map of Consciousness
Measured in Hertz

Enlightenment	700 - 1000
Peace	600
Gratitude	540
Joy	540
Love	500
Reason	400
Acceptance	350
Willingness	310
Neutrality	250
Courage	200
Pride	175
Anger	150
Desire	125
Fear	100
Grief	75
Apathy	50
Guilt	30
Shame	20

Reference David Hawkins, Power vs Force

Courage at 200 Hz is what shifts us from a slow, low frequency into a faster, higher frequency; therefore attracting money.

Have you ever heard someone say "high vibe" or "low vibe?" That isn't just cute slang for the 21st century, it's science.

Now, I want you to listen VERY CAREFULLY to this next part: it is NOT bad or wrong to experience a low vibration emotion.

There is absolutely zero need to feel afraid that your "bad atti-tude" or "feeling down" is going to keep you from making money.

Thinking that we need to stay high vibe, and then trying to stay high vibe, is a recipe for disaster. It's what's known as spiritual bypassing, or being Pollyanna.

In fact, avoiding, repressing, resisting, or ignoring feelings with a lower hertz measurement doesn't actually make you high vibe. That behavior secretly keeps you in a low vibration. It's like duct tape that isn't holding anything together.

The most helpful way to be with lower vibration emotions is to allow them, be with them, and process them.

For a reminder on how to process an emotion, visit chapter 14 for a step-by-step guide.

This is really a practice in allowing multiple things to be true at once. Or what I like to call "both/and."

It is necessary for us to feel and process lower vibration emotions, and it's the higher frequencies that attract money to us.

If you have a hard time wrapping your head around both of those things being true at once, play with this: being with and processing lower frequencies is what allows us to naturally be in a higher frequency where we are a money attractor.

Any of the emotions 200 hz and above activate our money magnet, and my personal favorite one to play with is joy.

I like to imagine money as a person to help understand how money follows joy. Imagine money, personified. Money wants a purpose and a party.

We wouldn't blame money for not hurrying over to hang out with shame, guilt, fear, or desperation. And it makes sense why money is RSVPing "yes" to any party that joy is at.

Joy can look like many different things. Reflecting on the top 3 energies in your Wealth Code will clue you in to the things that bring you the most joy.

Let's do a quick exercise to see how money follows joy for you.

The Joy Wheel
Make a list of all the things that you experience true joy around. This can be experiences, results, anything that you be/do/have.

-
-
-
-
-
-
-
-
-

For me, the things that bring me the most joy are when I am traveling, enjoying an incredible experience like horseback riding, a kayak ride, or an afternoon shopping, a new book, and when I'm with people I love.

Now, look at your list and ask yourself, "What's the common denominator? What is it about all of the things on my list that is joy-giving for me?"

We're looking for one simple word or phrase to sum it all up.

Hint: you might look at the top of your Wealth Code. It may be that word or something similar.

What's your common denominator?
- Connection with yourself, a higher power, or others
- Possibility
- Accomplishment
- Security and stability from self-respect
- Generosity
- Pleasure
- Celebration

When I look at my list of what gives me joy, I see the common denominator as a rich experience. For me, traveling, spending the day with a delightful activity, and being with people I love feels rich. And feeling that indulgent yumminess brings me so much joy.

The top of my Wealth Code is Pleasure and Celebration, so we can see how "rich experience" fits right in.

If Connection were the top of your Wealth Code, I would expect a common denominator of what brings you joy to be that you get to connect with yourself, a higher power, or other people.

If what brings you the most joy is winning a race and completing your to-do list, I would expect something like accomplishment to be your common denominator.

We call this common denominator your joy jumpstart. My joy jumpstart is "rich experiences." What's yours?

A few common joy jumpstarts that I've heard are things like: presence, deep connection, adventure, productivity, celebration, moments of bliss.

My joy jumpstart is: _____.

Now, when you are experiencing your joy jumpstart, what ACTION can you not help but take next? (Note: not, how do you feel, but what ACTION can you not help but take?)

My joy jumpstart is rich experiences and the action I can't help but take is to reflect in gratitude on how amazing the moment is. (Reflect is an action, not a feeling.)

Here's another example. If connection is your joy jumpstart, perhaps you can't help but take a photo to document the moment. (Taking a photo is an ACTION.)

What ACTION can you not help but take when you're experiencing your joy jumpstart? _____
_____

Now keep going with this same question: Then what ACTION can you not help but take next? _____
_____

Repeat that question, writing down your answer all the way until you can connect the dots that eventually, somewhere, somehow, joy leads you to money.

Here's a few things to consider:
If you're an entrepreneur, do you find that eventually you can't help but share about the way you help your clients and customers, and then you can't help but to grow your business, and then you can't help but make money?

If you work for someone else, do you find that eventually you cannot help but show up for work inspired to make a difference or do your job well, and then you can't help but receive a paycheck?

If you are in a relationship and you stay at home full time, with your partner receiving the paycheck, do you find that eventually you are a supportive partner who provides the ability for your significant other to work outside the home, and then you can't help but both benefit from that income?

If you don't receive money in the traditional way, do you eventually find that following your joy leads to money from unexpected and surprising places?

Here are a few examples for you to see.
Joy jumpstart: Rich Experiences > Reflect in gratitude on how amazing this moment is > Share about my experience > Connect with others who also like having rich experiences > Have conversations about how I could support them to create that in their lives > Grow my business > Make money

Example for an entrepreneur:
Joy jumpstart: Connection with myself, others, and God > Be present in the moment and soak it up > Take a photo to remember and look back on > Share the photo on social media > Be in conversation with others and hear about what they are doing > Offer my products to support what's going on in their lives > Make money

Example for someone who has a job working for a company:
Joy jumpstart: Being in a nature > Journal about thoughts I had > Be creative and follow my passions > Share with my family > Prioritize my family > Go to work to provide for my family > Receive a paycheck

Example for some who stays home full time and has a partner who receives the paycheck: Joy jumpstart: Accomplishing things around the house and with my family > Make a delicious meal to celebrate the day > Have conversations and support family members > Support my significant other while they go to work and I work at home > Celebrate the paycheck my significant other receives

Example if you always receive money unexpectedly or non-traditionally:
Joy jumpstart: Spontaneity > Stay present with this new experience > Consider what other experiences I might like to enjoy > Research and follow new threads > Make new connections > Stay open > Follow more threads > Make an invitation to help someone with a skill > Receive abundance in some form > Stay open > Receive money

Take a swing at making your own Joy Wheel. You might have anywhere from 5-8 action steps on your wheel. The key is to start with your joy jumpstart, the common denominator of "what brings me the most joy." And then at each answer ask, "What action can I not help but take next." Follow this wheel until it leads you to receiving money.

Joy always leads to money. The frequency of joy is so high that money just has to follow.

Joy Jumpstart

When I am "experiencing my joy jumpstart" I can't help but...

And then I can't help but...

And then I can't help but...

And then I can't help but...

And then I can't help but...

Chapter 20

Can't Afford it, or Not Being Resourceful?

Early in my education to become a coach I was sitting in a training session with my peers and one person was talking about how they couldn't afford to invest in something they really wanted.

I remember the lead trainer saying, "Is it that you can't afford it, or that you are not being resourceful?"

That question was powerful for me.

Until recently before this time in my life I was solidly in the camp of "I can't afford it." I missed out on things I really wanted all of the time because I was working to stretch $20 as far as it could go.

I thought if I didn't have the money in my bank account then the answer had to be no. End of story.

Until I learned about being resourceful. The truth is that the resources for ANYTHING we desire already exist. Quick exercise: think about any one of your desires. Does the money or resources that you'd need already exist somewhere in the world? The answer is yes :)

Sure, the money might not be in my bank account YET, but it could be. IF I am WILLING to be resourceful.

So that's what I started doing. Since that moment, I can't think of a single thing that I truly wanted that I haven't been able to give myself because of money (true story—I can show the receipts!).

And, being resourceful does not have to mean being scrappy and a hustler. Often, it's just about being courageous enough to tap into the resources available and hold myself as worthy enough to have my desires.

I'm sharing all of this with you because I want to invite you to be resourceful too. I'm committed to living in a world where every person gets that it's possible for them to have and pay for what they want, while staying in alignment.

I'm here for abundance for all. More is more. It's out there, are you willing to claim it?

By the way, this doesn't mean that just because you CAN create the resources for something doesn't mean you HAVE to. I could figure out a way to find the resources to buy a firetruck, but I'm not a firefighter, and I have no need or desire for a firetruck, so I won't.

The power is in knowing that it's not about whether or not the money is in your bank account, it's whether or not you'll access the resources when you are a yes for something. We get to let everything that we're a no for float right on by, it's not for us.

I'm going to share with you a list of 24 ways to be resourceful. There is a key ingredient to having any of these work for you:

being willing. If you are unwilling to take courageous action, or go out on the skinny part of the branch to get the fruit, it won't work.

This might be a time when we do not necessarily prefer to take courageous action because it would feel more comfortable to stay right where we are, but we are committed to having our desired result so we'll be willing to take action.

I want to share a story with you about one of the many times that I had to get willing.

When Tom and I had our offer accepted on our lake house, but we hadn't closed on it yet he asked me, "do you have the money to make the mortgage payment each month?"

The truth was that I was not setting aside that amount of money in an account every month and could now transfer it to our mortgage. In order for me to pay my half each month, I would need to create the money.

While I didn't have the money, I was willing. And that counts a lot more. I decided to play a game with myself. I wanted to make all of the money I'd need for a one month mortgage payment in one week. This would build my confidence by flexing into a new level of willingness.

I hopped on Facebook and shared an opportunity to go "camping" with me at a location to be announced in the town where we were buying our house. I called it "Camp YES" and put an investment of $500, which for two days of a retreat with me and all meals included was a great price. Typically, a one day VIP experience is an investment of $5,000+.

Within 24 hours I had sold all 10 spots.

It was a *bit* terrifying to offer this without even having the house where we'd be bringing everyone, but I knew that getting willing was the fastest path to success, and I was right.

I used some of the funds to cover the expenses for the weekend, and tucked the rest away for our first mortgage payment.

Being willing works.

Here's a list of 24 ways to be resourceful.
1. Use a credit card
2. Withdraw from a savings account
3. Enroll a new client
4. Pick up a dog sitting/house sitting job
5. Sell clothes/furniture you're ready to release
6. Collect on money from any debt owed to you
7. Pick up a house cleaning job
8. Offer to assist someone with a skill you have
9. Become an affiliate for a product or service you love
10. Make a referral and get paid a commission or sharing bonus
11. Use a line of credit or retirement fund
12. Monetize a hobby
13. Invite 5-10 people for a 1-day retreat on a topic you are passionate about
14. Create a package with a skillset you have and offer it to others
15. Ask someone to be your angel investor
16. Ask a friend for a gift or loan
17. Create a list of 10 ways that you can help people, ask to get hired for those things 18. Pick up a part-time job
19. Work for Lyft/Doordash, etc.
20. Use the money in your checking account
21. Make an easy offer to work with you at a savings

22. Invite someone who has been your client to renew and pay in full
23. Start a crowdfunding campaign
24. Ask someone if there is any house tasks they need help with

Which one of these will you try?

A few years ago, I was in the last session with a client for her coaching package. She told me that she'd really like to renew again, but it felt best to her to pay in full instead of making payments. And even though she'd like to renew, she couldn't afford it right now. The package we were working in was a $16,000 investment. She told me she didn't have that much money in any of her accounts combined.

I asked her, "What's the easiest, most delightful way to receive $16,000?" She said she was going to stay open for that answer to be revealed to her.

Thirty minutes later she called me back, "I have the money" she said. I smiled. That was easy. I asked her what the answer turned out to be. She told me that she has a personal training client she's been working with for years who always pays one session at a time, but could easily afford to pay for a package in full. She called him and shared that she was wanting to make an investment in herself, and if he could pay for a certain number of sessions up front it would help her.

He agreed right away. He knew that he was going to continue working with her and was delighted to help her make an investment in herself. She was on her way to pick up a check.

It can be that easy, if we let it be.

I know, I know, you're saying "must be nice, but I don't have a job or a client like that. I can't just tell people I need $16,000 and they'll hand it to me."

Maybe not. But you do have the ability to be resourceful. You can ask yourself, "What's the easiest, most delightful way to receive the money I am looking for?"

You can stay open to the answer that comes and be courageous to follow it through. Consider that my client didn't think that was possible for her either, until she did.

And maybe you've tried, hundreds, thousands, or millions (but probably not) of times to tap into a resource and it didn't work.

Try a new resource. Shift your frequency. Be open rather than angry. (You're allowed to be angry, it's just not the space to receive money. Process your anger, then shift back to neutrality and openness. This is where you and money will meet.)

Tapping into resources is the path to affording what we want.

Chapter 21

Places We Get Stuck: Time

Another of the three most common places that we get stuck is around time. Time objections sound like, "I don't have enough time." "I'm too busy." "My schedule is maxed." "I'm overwhelmed as it is." "It's not a good time." "I need to wait until X is finished."

Just like with money, if someone told me any of these things, I would believe them. And, I'd be curious about the deeper truth at play that these circumstances with time are a symptom of.

Time objections surface when our proximity to possibility is getting a little too close for comfort. If there is a part of us that is fearful or apprehensive of a new possibility or a change occurring it will try to pump the brakes to keep us from getting to that place. The way we pump the brakes is by saying, "I just don't have the time."

Change can be scary. Even if it's the change we've been wanting. Even if we say, "I love change." A change in one area of life will ripple into other areas, and that's often where the fear can sneak in.

I've seen this exact rumble with a time objection more than I can count. An entrepreneur has been working to grow their business for a while, and even if they make a bit of traction, overall they feel like they haven't tapped into the results they really desire yet.

They've tried so many things, invested in a number of courses, and still feel like their wheels are spinning. Also, they are busy. They are busy doing busy work to "get ready to get ready." Things like making sure their logo looks just how they want. Listening to a new podcast and trying to get their own off the ground. Putting ideas on paper for the next course they can run.

And when we get curious and honest about what's really going on, we usually come to a place like this: "I am afraid that if I actually had all of the clients that I desire that I would be too busy for my family. I would miss out on things because I had a meeting, or I wouldn't be able to make dinner because I was finishing something up for work."

We can see that staying busy keeps them available. We can set our work, fine-tuning our logo aside if we need to make a quick trip to the vet. And we can wrap up the brainstorming on a future course when the kids get home from school and it's time for dinner.

Being busy can be a protection against the change of having a fully-booked business.

Now that's just one example. Your dance with time might look different. Here are some other common things we've discovered to be the root of a time objection.

- If I really followed my dreams I'd make a lot more money, and then I'm not sure if my relationships would stay the same (so maybe this isn't the right time.)
- If I decided to really have what I want I'd need to get out of my comfort zone, and I'm not sure that feels good (so it's a good thing I'm too busy.)

- Being a yes to what I want would require me to make an investment, and I don't even want to face the rejection from my bank account telling me that I don't have the funds (but it doesn't matter because my schedule is maxed.)
- If I said yes to this desire I would have to add more onto my plate, and I am terrified of drowning in overwhelm, I don't think my body can handle it (I'm overwhelmed as it is.) If I went for it I know that I'd need to change some of my personal patterns or beliefs, and I'm not sure that I'm ready for that (so I just need to wait.)
- Even though I want to, I can't. There are other commitments and priorities that need my attention (I just need to wait until X is done.) Which is convenient because I actually don't want to take on the responsibility of following through with this.

Do you see a past or current version of you in any of this?

I am certainly not exempt from getting stopped by any of these objections. I don't think that any human is.

Let me tell you about a time that I got a phone call from my grandma who told me that her doctor recommended that she go on the Whole30 diet for 30 days. I had never heard of this, so I did a quick google search. As I was reading about the Whole30 I was wholly overwhelmed. There were (in my opinion then) so many foods that you had to eliminate for 30 days. It felt totally impossible and like it would be very challenging to eat anything.

This initial conversation happened in the summer, let's say June or July. Even though this had been a recommendation for my grandma, through my research a number of things stood out to me that had me thinking that this would actually be really good for me too. I was having a lot of digestive symptoms, headaches constantly, weight gain, acne; all things I read could be improved while on the Whole30. I said to myself, "I could never do this. I'm too busy and wouldn't be able to eat anything at the places I'm going to."

So, I delayed. I stopped myself thinking that this wasn't the right time. For the next six months my symptoms continued to intensify. As the end of the year approached, and I couldn't stop thinking about what I had read about the Whole30 I decided that I was going to commit to it.

Tom had recently moved in with me and he is a whizz in the kitchen, so I knew that I'd have support figuring out what to eat. I enrolled Tom and my best friend to complete the Whole30 with me in the month of January.

The January that I completed the Whole30 was one of the most pivotal points in my life. Quickly many of the physical symptoms that I had been experiencing improved. I thought with amazement to myself, "I really thought everyone had a stomach ache at the end of the day, but apparently not."

I began to experience clarity in my life like never before. This was the month that I courageously enrolled in the $16,500 coaching and leadership program without knowing how I'd pay for it. I am certain that having courageously committed to the Whole30 and figuring it out gave me a spirited boost to believe in myself with this too.

I ended up releasing dairy, and most gluten from my life (I go wild for three ingredient homemade sourdough and am grateful to say that after years of healing my gut, my body now loves it too).

I'm coming up on nine years of having these changes be my lifestyle. The Whole30 opened the door to more changes as well. This was a point when I felt like I was really coming "online" with my intuition, which led me to the decision to eat plant-based. And the changes just kept rolling from there.

Side note: I'm not here to be an evangelist for the Whole30 or a plant-based diet. I'm sharing my own personal experience. Perhaps you'll be inspired to see something in this for yourself, and perhaps what is aligned for your body is totally different than mine. Yay, I celebrate that. And, if you've been curious, maybe this is a nudge to explore it for yourself.

The point of my story: I got in my own way thinking that it wasn't the right time*, and when I got out of my way, I changed my life.

Now, we need to address something very important: the little asterisk I put after "I got in my own way thinking that it wasn't the right time." I believe everything I just said above, and I believe this: I don't think it was the right time, when I first heard about it.

It's not bad or wrong to have an objection. It's not "right" to see an objection and immediately hurdle over it. During those six months I was undoubtedly doing the inner work of building the trust inside myself to commit to a transformation like this. I likely would have failed had I tried to start right away.

So how do we know when it's "the right time?" When we decide to go.

Sometimes the breakthrough comes in moving beyond an objection. And sometimes the breakthrough comes from temporarily empowering the objection.

This, empowering the objection, is a regular practice for me. If I'm up against an objection, rather than trying to pretend that I'm a victim to the circumstance I'll own that I'm choosing the objection.

Instead of the victim-y response: "I can't because I'm too busy" I empower the objection: "I'm not willing to change that yet."

When we say "it's not the right time," or "I'm too busy," we're giving time all the power. When we say "I'm not willing," we're keeping the power within ourselves. I am making a choice. It may not be the choice I'll make for forever, but it's the choice I'm making right now. By acknowledging that it's a choice, we're also acknowledging that we could choose something differently.

Objections are really bumping up against our willingness. Our willingness to stand in our worthiness, our willingness for new possibilities, our willingness to trust ourselves. If there is any part of us that is hesitant about that, it throws up an objection to slow us down.

When I'm coaching someone who is feeling so maxed around time, it's typically not that they need to become a scheduling wizard who completes everything on their schedule and nothing else. Honestly, that's unrealistic. I work with a lot of parents and leaders of organizations who are going to have urgent requests and things that need their attention. It's not going to work to expect them to only do what's on their calendar and ignore the rest of life.

Just so we're clear: if you are feeling that you never have enough time, more organization (alone) isn't the solution.

You need to be willing. Willing to have things go differently. Willing for something that has been your responsibility to now be someone else's. Willing to have more of what you really want, and less of all the tasks, and to-dos that you currently have.

One of the simple practices I like to take on when I'm noticing things are piling up on my to-do list is called Do, Delegate, Delete. Let's try it together right now.

Do, Delegate, Delete

Get a piece of paper and make 3 columns. Label one "do," one "delegate", and one "delete."

Now you're going to assign all of the things that have been on your mental or written to-do list to one of these three columns. When I play, I try to have an even number in each column. So if I'm going to put three things on my "do" list, I'm also going to put three things on the "delegate" list and three things on the "delete" list.

Let me give you a few tips. The things that you are keeping on your "do" list are what absolutely is necessary to be done by you, and the things that give you the greatest joy. You'll likely find that a lot of what goes on this list are things that involve your own self-care. Someone else can't go on a run for you in order for you to get the benefits.

The things you put on your delegate list are what need to be done, and you can have support from someone else. This is a space where you can get creative. Perhaps there is a partner or team member who can help you out. Or maybe even Chat GPT depending on what it is. You may need someone to come in and complete the project right next to you so that if you are needed you'll be there, but your energy is largely freed up.

I could put almost anything on the delegate list with enough willingness and creativity. The key here is really to be creative. When I was in college, and the year I lived in an apartment complex with friends nearby after college, we delegated dinners to each other. I would make dinner for my friend and I on Tuesday, and she would make it on Thursday. This way each of us had one night a week we didn't have to have "make dinner" on our to-do list. Now my husband makes all of our meals. He meal plans, grocery shops, and prep cooks everything on Sunday. For the rest of the week, neither of us have this on our to-do list.

In the early days of my coaching practice I mostly met with my clients in person. One of my clients was a single mom with two small boys. Sometimes we'd meet for her sessions in the lobby of my YMCA so that she could use the two hours of free day care service they provide to members each day as long as the parent is on site. That was a great way to be creative!

And the last thing is delete. This is where we let go of anything that really is not of highest service for us to take on right now. That might mean that we delegate someone else to pick up baked goods for us to bring to the potluck instead of us baking them on our own.

Or, this means saying to yourself, "I know that I thought organizing my closet was a priority, and right now I am going to take that off of my list."

Do, delegate, delete is so helpful because instead of having a long list of to-dos, we'll free up our energy to focus on what matters most.

Just remember, the key to all of this is willingness. When we are willing for things to be different, we can open up to an expansive experience of time. When we are feeling maxed for time, it's a sign that we are in resistance and unwilling to have things be different.

Feeling stuck? That's exactly the kind of inner work that is so supportive to do with a coach. When we can dig into what's going on with your beliefs and willingness, we can open up new possibilities.

Do

_____

_____

_____

_____

_____

_____

Delegate

_____

_____

_____

_____

_____

_____

Delete

_____

_____

_____

_____

_____

_____

Chapter 22

Places We Get Stuck: Approval

The third of the most common places that we get stuck when on a way to being a yes for ourselves and our dreams is around approval. Approval can look like both approval from another person, and approval from a circumstance.

When seeking approval from another person we are often checking in with a spouse, business partner, parent, child, accountant, financial advisor, boss, etc.

When seeking approval from a circumstance we might be looking for something like our tax refund, a bonus, our schedule, etc. Approval from a circumstance means that if this other thing goes like I think it will, then I can keep moving forward, but if it doesn't, I'm going to be stopped.

This can sound like, "I'm just waiting to see how much of a tax return I'm getting. If it's big enough to cover the payment for this then I can do it."

Approval doesn't have to mean that you are forbidden to do it unless you get the pre-approval. We can also think of it as checking in, seeing what they say, making sure that we're on the same page, etc.

Sometimes we downplay approval by calling it another name, something softer like, "I'm going to see what they think about this." And the essence of that is that we are seeking approval.

We don't often like to think of ourselves as explicitly getting approval from someone or something, but I see it all of the time. Just like with money and time, the need for approval really isn't about approval at all, it's about trust.

If I'm not fully trusting myself then I will seek the green light from someone/something else. I'll say that "I need to check in with XYZ" but what I'm really doing is avoiding trusting the decision that I would make for myself.

This is one of the sneakiest ways that we sabotage ourselves. We use other people and circumstances as scapegoats so that we don't have to be in trust, or with any consequences of that trust.

We tend to have a lot of women joining our coaching programs. It's not unusual to hear in an enrollment conversation they say something like, "This is so great. I'm really excited. I'm just going to check with my husband that he is on board."

If we translate that, what she's really saying is, "I want to choose this, but I'm leery of trusting myself. I'm afraid that if I invest this money and don't show up to create the result that I want then I'm going to be disappointed and my partner might be too. I want to avoid that feeling."

Instead of avoiding that feeling by being in full trust and then showing up and following through, the path that many people choose is to "check in" with someone else so that they can share the blame.

When we get approval from someone else what we're really saying is, "I don't want you to be disappointed if I don't get the intended result. Can we agree now that we'll share the blame if this doesn't go as planned so I don't have to feel bad?"

This is problematic on many levels. First, there doesn't need to be any blame. Second, we don't need to be secretly inviting our partners to be complicit in us not creating our intended results. Third, instead of planning for us to not have what we want, let's focus on trusting ourselves to create what we do.

It's not fair to our partners or whoever we're seeking approval from to be put in this spot. Whether they know it or not, they are reading our energy when we come to them asking for their insight. If we are in a state of mistrust, they are going to pick up on that and also wonder if this is really the best choice for us.

It's manipulative to put the decision on someone else so that we can avoid having to trust ourselves and be with the responsibility and consequences of our choice.

We use circumstances in the same way. Instead of making a choice based truly on if it's in alignment for us and if we trust ourselves, we use whatever external circumstance as the scapegoat.

It's such a bummer to let a pending tax refund give us the green light instead of our own self-trust.

Now, I know that was a fire hose of truth being poured all over you. Some of you may be sitting here saying, "Oh no, I trust myself, it's just that my partner and I have an agreement that we always make decisions together, especially over $X."

Let me start by saying that I am not in your partnership and any agreements you have made are none of my business. And, since we've agreed that at least through the duration of this book I am going to be your life coach, I'm going to ask some coaching questions on that topic.

If you and your partner have an agreement that you always make decisions together, what is that in service of?

Really, I'm asking, "How come you and your partner always make decisions together?"

Listen, your answer is your business. Different strokes for different folks. I'd also like to offer the perspective that I've seen couples create that agreement because there is one partner who doesn't trust themselves, and therefore the other partner doesn't trust them either. If that's what's going on it's worth looking at. Is that the most powerful kind of dynamic to have within a partnership?

I am not saying that you need to throw everything out the window and have a free for all where each person just makes any choices they see fit for their partner to find out about or not. That's also not an empowered partnership.

Here's a new option. Rather than going to your partner for approval, have a conversation where you share with them the decision that you are making for yourself and ask if they trust you in it. Woah, can you feel how big that is? It's big.

Let's play this out in a scenario. We're going to pretend that Mary has decided she is going to start renting a studio space to bring her dream of becoming an artist to life. She's going to have a conversation with her husband, Jim.

Scenario 1, asking for approval.

Mary: Hey Jim, I've been thinking that I really want my own studio space for my art. It's been going well at home but I'm wanting to spread out more and not have to clean up at the end of every day. I found this studio space for $1,000/month. I really want to do it, but it also feels like a lot of money every month. I think eventually I'll be able to sell way more than that in art and classes each month, but at first I'm not sure how it will go. I'll probably need a bit of an adjustment period. I don't want that $1,000 to feel like a burden for the family. I know we have a vacation coming up and the kids need new bikes this year too, not to mention all of the other things for their summer activities. What do you think? I want to do it but I'm kind of afraid.

Now, Jim both hears Mary's desire, but also all of her fear. He's reminded of all the expenses and also doesn't want to bear the responsibility of an extra $1,000 expense. Either he supports her because he can see what she's capable of, or he supports her conditionally, meaning that he says he supports having the studio space if she can find a way to pay for it every month. Or, he doesn't support her because he's also afraid of that extra expense.

Any way this goes, it's not empowering for Mary. Rather than trusting herself, she's caught between desire and fear and ultimately makes whichever choice based on Jim's level of comfort, not her own trust.

Scenario 2, sharing trust.

Mary: Hey Jim, I've made a decision that I'm really excited about. I want to share it with you and ask that you'll trust me and support the way that I'm trusting myself. I've decided that I'm going to rent an art studio. This is really important to me because I know that having this space is going to be a key in my growth personally, as an artist, and in the way that I can open up to receiving more money selling my work and teaching classes. It's $1,000 per month. This is a business expense, and in the coming months my art business will be able to cover it completely. I realize that while I get adjusted, I may personally need to pay the rent for a few months, and that makes sense because there is often a personal investment that comes when starting a business. I know that we have a vacation coming up and other expenses for the kids. My intention is that as I have the space to grow, my business can contribute to the family's expenses. Is there anything else that you'd need to hear from me so that you can support me and the way that I'm trusting myself?

Here, Jim has the space to share any of his feelings. He can support Mary completely, he can ask questions, he can also share any fears that he has. There can be dialogue and commitments made by Mary and Jim so that both partners feel good around Mary's decision.

There is so much power in being able to be in harmony with our patterns while rooted in self trust. When we ask our partners to trust and support us we are growing and expanding our relationship. This creates a strong foundation.

Trusting ourselves, and inviting others to trust us, creates more trust.

Passing our trust to someone else to make decisions for us keeps us in a state of being disconnected from our worthiness. If you are in a space of both looking for approval and feeling like you don't have the money it's a double whammy of trust and connection to worth. One feeds into the next. Give yourself the gift of connecting to your worth so that you can trust yourself, and trust yourself so that you can connect with your worth.

Here are a few practices that you can take on to flex your self trust muscle:

1. Practice hearing and listening to your intuition. Trust it for small things like ordering new food at a restaurant or taking a different route when driving somewhere.
2. Ask "What's the best that could happen?" Follow that.
3. Give yourself an hour with no agenda, trust yourself to create value in that hour by pouring into you with whatever feels best.
4. Make a commitment to yourself to take a small but powerful action every day for a certain number of days. For example, commit to flossing your teeth every day for 7 days, or starting your morning with a glass of lemon water every day for 30 days.
5. Make a decision and follow it all the way through.

Chapter 23

Alone or Deeply Supported?

As we move through all of these ideas and resources to bring us closer to being a yes for ourselves there is one big thing that we haven't covered yet: control.

Control keeps us spinning where we are. I can totally understand the allure of control. Trust me, I love when I get to say how everything will go, and then everything goes that way. Which, I think both of us know, never really happens.

As much as we'd like to have everything go according to our magic wand, life doesn't work that way. The more that we try to control, the more that we isolate ourselves.

Control can come in all shapes and sizes. It can look like "do-it-myself-itis." It can look like "wait-for-things-to-be-perfect-ville" or, "only-when-I'm-ready-ness."

What's your favorite flavor of control? Personally, I tend toward "it's all on me." And what I know for a fact is that "it's all on me" doesn't work.

Control leaves us vulnerable to circumstances. My friend, circumstances will always come. But there's a remedy to control, it's called being deeply supported.

There's an analogy I like to use to demonstrate the disadvantages of control and the power of support…

Let's imagine that you're alone on an island. Things will go exactly how you say they'll go, and you get to do them all yourself. So you find the wood and make a fire, you forage for berries to eat, and when it starts to rain, you hold your own umbrella over the fire to make sure the rain doesn't put it out. You might be able to do all of the things, but you cannot do them all at the same time. You will get in your own way.

When we are trying to control everything, circumstances slow us down, and keep us from having it all.

Now imagine that you're on an island, and you're the leader of your life. You have a team there to support you. You get to delegate: someone gets firewood, someone else forages for berries, and when it rains someone holds an umbrella over the fire, and you get to hold an umbrella over yourself so you can stay warm by the fire while eating your berries. You get to have it all being supported.

I know that is an extremely oversimplified analogy, but it demonstrates for us how limiting trying to be in control actually is. When we are trying to control everything, we are not allowing ourselves to be deeply supported.

Control operates in scarcity. Power, which is a way of being, is rooted in abundance and comes from allowing ourselves to be supported.

How has it been going for you so far? Have you been trying to control everything; your finances, your schedule, and those around you?

What if you allowed yourself to be deeply supported? What is possible when you open up to the gifts and talents of others helping you get where you want to go.

Here's what I know for sure: you have everything inside of you to have your dreams come true.

I also know that we can bring our dreams to life faster, easier, and while having way more fun when we let ourselves be supported. This is why I want to stand for you to have a coach.

Working with a life coach holds up a mirror so that you can see what's in your blind spot. Having that awareness then puts you at choice to have beliefs and take actions that are in your highest service.

Whatever it is that you want to create in your life will be supported by having a coach who is rooting for you, standing for you, creating accountability, and celebrating with you.

Every incredible athlete has a coach. They have someone in their corner holding them to their greatness. You deserve to be held to your greatness too.

Along with having someone in our corner for support and accountability, I find that having a structure for how we'll be accountable to showing up for ourselves is very helpful.

The structure that we find supportive is made of four pillars:
- Daily moments of intention (connect with your desires, possibility)

- Weekly connection (we're made to be in community)
- Monthly pattern interruption (this is what we do in coaching)
- Quarterly deep dives (focusing on one area to support our growth)

We've designed all of our coaching offers around these four pillars. We know that this is a support and accountability structure that works to move our clients forward toward their dreams.

For example, this could look like:
- Daily receiving a pocket coaching text message to have you reflect and reconnect with what you are committed to.
- Attending group coaching sessions each week so that you can be supported alongside others who are walking this journey too.
- Having a 1:1 coaching session each month so that your coach can hold up a mirror and interrupt any patterns that have been in your blind spots, and together you can create a shift.
- Identifying one place that you can create a breakthrough to open you up to the next level of abundance in whichever area of life you feel most called.

This is exactly the kind of support that we provide our clients. The proof is in the pudding! Aka the amazing lives our clients who show up and let themselves be supported get to live.

Visit RiseLeadershipCircle.com/Yes for more information on how to work with us.

If you're thinking, "Great, I can create all of these for myself!"

Yes, you can. I offer this…You totally can. *And*, will it serve you the most? Does that keep you in a place of control, or being supported?

Letting yourself be deeply supported is a choice. Living your YES life is a choice too. I find the people who choose to be deeply supported also choose, and live their YES life the quickest, and forever.

What will you choose?

Chapter 24

Be a YES for YOU

Let's put a bow on this, baby! While the book is ending, your YES life is just beginning. There are so many possibilities of where you go from here.

I want to close with a few powerful reminders, some key coaching questions, and acknowledgment of you.

Powerful reminders:
1. You are the only expert of your life.
2. You get to have any experience of life that you decide.
3. Circumstances (like money, time, or approval) are not your boss. You are the authority of your life and get to make powerful decisions, bringing the circumstances along for the ride.
4. The fastest way to have what you want is to be deeply connected to your worthiness, embrace possibility, and stand in self-trust.
5. The things that we let slow us down the most are money, time, and thinking we need approval. But it's never actually about those things. We pretend money is the reason we can't have what we want when what's really going on

is that we've disconnected from our worth. Time seems to be getting in our way when we're actually pumping the brake on possibility. We seek approval when we are not trusting ourselves.

6. You are worthy of your desires and dreams.
7. You get to choose what you say yes to.

Coaching Questions:

1. What dream are you choosing to be a yes for?
2. What will it look like to embody your worth while creating that dream?
3. What possibilities do you get to be willing to embrace while creating that dream?
4. What will it look like to trust yourself while creating that dream?
5. Who is the authority on your life?
6. Would having a coach be supportive to help keep you committed to your yes, out of your own way, and in powerful action while creating your dream?
7. What is the next action for you to take?

Acknowledgment:

Dear you,

You are worthy of so much celebration. You've made it here! You have loved yourself enough to pick up this book and read it cover to cover. You've taken on the practices and looked at some things inside of yourself that you may have not known to look at previously.

You connected with your worth, explored possibilities, and activated self-trust.

You *are* the person that you are here to be. You are a gift to this world. Shining your light is your birthright.

Go get your yeses, and then some!

Photographer, Kate McFadzen-Lindsay

Life Coach, entrepreneur, and author Kaela Gedda has taken her personal experience of *wanting* life to look different, and transformed her reality into one of saying YES to her biggest dreams.

Kaela is the Co-founder of Rise Leadership Circle, who along with the best partner a girl could ask for, her mom Lisa Liimatta, provides Life Coaching and transformation to heart-centered leaders, entrepreneurs, and visionaries. She also is the Co-founder of The Nest Cowork + Club in her hometown of Green Bay, WI.

Kaela has a background in sales both with for-and-nonprofit organizations. As a Life Coach, she helps her clients gain clarity on their deepest desires and then bring them to life creating lasting fulfillment.

She is regularly featured on stage at leadership conferences, on podcasts to share about her journey from being six figures in debt to becoming a six-figure-earner in her first year of entrepreneurship, and in publications like Goss Magazine. You can also hear her on the podcast that she co-hosts; Live Your YES Life.

Kaela lives with her husband, Tom, and their three dogs: Murray, Mildred, and Melvin, between their two homes in Wisconsin and on the lake in the Upper Peninsula of Michigan. Her favorite activities are kayaking, being with animals in nature, and an afternoon at the spa.

You can learn more about working with Kaela at RiseLeadership-Circle.com/Yes

www.ingramcontent.com/pod-product-compliance
Lightning Source LLC
Chambersburg PA
CBHW070325130626
46556CB00007B/2741